D0849481

**DATE DUE**

| 11 March 2014 | | | |
|---|---|---|---|
| | | | |
| | | | |
| | | | |
| | | | |
| | | | |
| | | | |
| | | | |
| | | | |
| | | | |
| | | | |
| | | | |
| | | | |
| | | | |
| | | | |
| | | | |
| | | | |

# NORWAY

**ABDO**
Publishing Company

# NORWAY

*by Carol Hand*

**Content Consultant**
Margaret Hayford O'Leary, PhD
Professor, Chair of Norwegian Department, Saint Olaf College

# CREDITS

Published by ABDO Publishing Company, PO Box 398166, Minneapolis, MN 55439. Copyright © 2013 by Abdo Consulting Group, Inc. International copyrights reserved in all countries. No part of this book may be reproduced in any form without written permission from the publisher. The Essential Library™ is a trademark and logo of ABDO Publishing Company.

Printed in the United States of America,
North Mankato, Minnesota
112012
012013

 THIS BOOK CONTAINS AT LEAST 10% RECYCLED MATERIALS.

Editor: Erika Wittekind
Series Designer: Emily Love

About the Author: Carol Hand has a PhD in zoology. She has taught college biology, written biology assessments for national assessment companies, written middle- and high-school science curricula for a national company, and authored young-adult books on science and other topics. She works as a freelance writer of nonfiction for young adults.

**Cataloging-in-Publication Data**

Hand, Carol.
 Norway / Carol Hand.
   p. cm. -- (Countries of the world)
Includes bibliographical references and index.
ISBN 978-1-61783-633-6
1. Norway--Juvenile literature.   I. Title.
948.1--dc22

                                                    2012946074

**Cover:  The Geirangerfjord in Norway is surrounded by mountain peaks and waterfalls.**

# TABLE OF CONTENTS

# CHAPTER 1
# A VISIT TO NORWAY

Your trip of a lifetime is about to begin! Norway is one of the world's most expensive countries, so you've been saving all year for this trip. You are excited to see Norway's natural beauty, especially glaciers and fjords. Since it's summer, you will even get to experience the midnight sun.

But before you begin, your tour guide gives the group some insight into the Norwegian character. She tells you Norwegians are friendly, but tend to be less open and outgoing than most Americans. They are polite and dislike confrontation, shouting, or causing a scene. But they can also be very funny, with a dry sense of humor, and are ready to have fun when the occasion presents itself.

Your tour begins in Oslo, Norway's capital, which appears prosperous. The guide reminds you that Norway's wealth is due to the discovery of oil in the North Sea in the 1960s. Smaller than most capital cities, Oslo is Norway's largest city and its intellectual and cultural center.

**Pulpit Rock at Lysefjorden, one of Norway's most well-known tourist destinations, towers 1,969 feet (600 m) above sea level.**

## THE OSLO OPERA HOUSE

The Oslo Opera House is set on the waters of Oslo Fjord. Its outer shell of brilliant white Italian marble resembles an iceberg. Numerous horizontal and sloping marble rooftops, called the Carpet, serve as a public space. Visitors enter the building under a low ceiling and move gradually into a vast foyer. On one side, 49-foot (15 m) windows flood the area with light.[1] Aluminum structural columns, perforated to resemble icicles and glaciers, reflect light both inside and outside the building. Within the foyer is the massive Wave Wall, strips of golden oak curved into organic shapes. A grand staircase leads to three seating galleries and other rooms. Shifting light conveys ever-changing patterns throughout the days and seasons.

Your first stop is the new Oslo Opera House, which resembles an iceberg. When you walk up the slope of the building's shiny white, multilevel rooftop, you are surprised to see people sunbathing. It's clear Norwegians take advantage of sun wherever they find it. Inside, the building is even more impressive. Its vast, light-filled foyer and curving oak staircase soar above you.

Over the next few days, you visit several of Oslo's first-class museums—several art museums, the Viking Ship Museum, and the Holmenkollen Ski Museum. The museums give a real sense of history. You might find it hard to believe the three huge oaken Viking ships were built more than 1,000 years ago. And before seeing how explorers used skis to cross Greenland and Antarctica for the first time, you might have thought of skiing as a sport, not as a means of transportation.

**The distinctive Oslo Opera House opened in 2008.**

In the evenings, your group walks through Oslo's downtown. Even late at night, it's still light outside, and people are playing soccer and bicycling along city trails. Later, at Oslo's nightspots, you fit in easily and discover that Norway's young people are not that different from you. They seem more casual and open than their elders, and are even knowledgeable about American television and movies.

# ARCTIC ADVENTURE

The rest of Norway is very different from Oslo. To get a more complete picture, the group takes the Bergen Railway—a daylong train ride from Oslo to Bergen across the widest part of the country. Bergen is a cool, rainy west coast town where you will begin the highlight of your trip—a 12-day round-trip cruise along the west coast to experience the fjords and the Arctic summer. The ferry is a combined cruise/cargo ship that travels north and then east, stopping at 34 ports. It follows Norway's western and northern boundaries far above the Arctic Circle to Kirkenes, where Norway connects with Finland and Russia. As the ship travels along the coast, you drink in the beauty and peacefulness of the scenery. You also take innumerable photos and videos of fjords, waterfalls, and islands. Giant vertical cliffs tower above the ferry on either side as you pass through fjords. Cruising north toward Kristiansund, you pass many groups

## THE BERGEN RAILWAY

The Bergen Railway from Oslo to Bergen is considered by some to be the most beautiful and exciting train ride in Europe. It reaches an altitude of 4,009 feet (1,222 m) above sea level at Finse. The seven-hour trip takes you past untouched forests, mountain wilderness, and incredible lakes and waterfalls. The highlight is a 12-mile (20 km) detour on the Flåm Railway at Myrdal, one of the world's steepest railway lines. It goes down to the tiny village of Flåm, at the tip of Aurlandfjord.[2]

**Bergen, Norway, is a popular cruise destination.**

of islands and skerries. It's hard to believe how clean and unspoiled everything looks.

An unforgettable stop in Trondheim is the Nidaros Cathedral, Norway's largest medieval cathedral. It was built on the grave of Saint

**The globe at the North Cape is a symbol of the northernmost point in continental Europe.**

Olaf. As you cross the Arctic Circle, you learn about the midnight sun phenomenon. The farther north you go, the more days of 24-hour sunlight there are per year. On the Svalbard Archipelago, there is constant sunlight from April 19 to August 23. It's weird to stand on the deck of the ship and see the sun throughout the night! Farther north is Tromsø, the northernmost Norwegian city, where the sun never sets in the summer and the activity continues all night. You arrive just in time for the annual Midnight Sun Marathon. During the day, your tour group visits the Polaria, a multimedia museum that teaches about the Arctic, and the Mack Brewery, which dates from 1877.

In Arctic Norway the word *nature* takes on a whole new meaning. Even from the ship, you catch glimpses of Norway's wildlife—a pod of orcas fishing for herring, huge racks of cod drying on the Lofoten Islands, and rookeries of thousands of sea birds—puffins and gannets—nesting off the coast of Finnmark.

## LAND OF THE MIDNIGHT SUN

During the summer, the sun never sets from the Arctic Circle northward to the North Pole. From late May through mid-August, there are 24 hours of daylight and no true darkness. The farther north you travel, the more days the 24-hour daylight lasts. Tourists visit the region specifically to see this phenomenon. In the depths of winter, the same region experiences one to two months of nearly 24-hour darkness every day, with a brief twilight in the middle of the day.

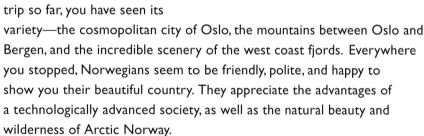

You might have expected all of Norway to be fairly similar. But on your trip so far, you have seen its variety—the cosmopolitan city of Oslo, the mountains between Oslo and Bergen, and the incredible scenery of the west coast fjords. Everywhere you stopped, Norwegians seem to be friendly, polite, and happy to show you their beautiful country. They appreciate the advantages of a technologically advanced society, as well as the natural beauty and wilderness of Arctic Norway.

**Political Boundaries of Norway**

# SNAPSHOT

Official name: Kingdom of Norway (Norwegian: Kongeriket Norge)

Capital city: Oslo

Form of government: constitutional monarchy

Title of leaders: king (chief of state); prime minister (head of government)

Currency: Norwegian kroner

Population (July 2012 est.): 4,707,270
*World rank:* 120

Size: 125,021 square miles (323,802 sq km)
*World rank:* 68

Language: Bokmål Norwegian, Nynorsk Norwegian

Official religion: none

Per capita GDP (2011, US dollars): $54,200
*World rank:* 8

# CHAPTER 2
# GEOGRAPHY: TOP OF THE WORLD

Norway is a country of the far north, and one-third of its land mass lies above the Arctic Circle. Long, thin, and spoon shaped, it is less than five miles (8 km) wide in some places. It clings to the northwestern coast of Scandinavia, in northern Europe. Its eastern land boundary touches three countries. The longest border—1,006 miles (1,619 km)—is with Sweden. North of Sweden, a 452-mile (727 km) length borders Finland; above that, a 122-mile (196 km) section borders Russia.[1] To the west is the North Atlantic Ocean. In this region, it is called the Norwegian Sea. The North Sea surrounds its southern tip, separating it from the tiny country of Denmark. Norway's area also includes more than 50,000 small islands and the Svalbard Archipelago, a large group of islands 400 miles (644 km) north of the Norwegian mainland in the Barents Sea, which is part of the Arctic Ocean.[2]

**The dual waterfall Låtefossen is located in the Odda Valley in western Norway.**

The entire west coast of Norway is indented with deep, fingerlike fjords. Although its total eastern land boundary measures only approximately 1,578 miles (2,542 km) from south to north, the length of Norway's coastline with its fjords is more than 15,626 miles (25,148 km). Island coastlines add another 36,122 miles (58,133 km).[3]

The country's total land area is 125,021 square miles (323,802 sq km), making it larger than New Mexico but smaller than California.[4] The northern and eastern regions are mostly unpopulated, and a backbone of snowy mountains—the Scandinavian Mountains, or the Keel—runs down the country's center.

Norway's largest city is the capital, Oslo, which had a metropolitan population of 875,000 as of 2009.[5] Norway's other cities and towns are much smaller, and most are spread along the coastline. Other important cities are Bergen, Trondheim, and

## GLACIERS

More than 1,004 square miles (2,600 sq km) of Norway, including 60 percent of Svalbard, is covered by glaciers. Jostedals Glacier, the largest glacier on the European mainland, is located in the Western Fjords region, near the northern part of the country's "spoon." It has an area of 188 square miles (487 sq km) and makes up one-half of Jostedalsbreen National Park. Smaller but still impressive glaciers on the Norwegian mainland include Folgefonna and Svartisen. But the island of Svalbard wins the prize for Norway's—and Europe's—largest glacier. Austfonna, with a front 656 feet (200 m) across, is the world's third-largest ice sheet, after Antarctica and Greenland.[6]

**Jostedals Glacier is the largest glacier on the European mainland.**

Stavanger. The largest town in northern Norway is Tromsø, far above the Arctic Circle.

## NORWAY'S LANDFORMS

A massive ice sheet covered Norway during the last Ice Age. Beginning approximately 10,000 years ago, the melting and retreating ice carved out deep U-shaped valleys that connected to the sea. These valleys, with their extremely steep, narrow sides, filled with salt water and became fjords. Their rugged natural beauty draws millions of tourists to Norway

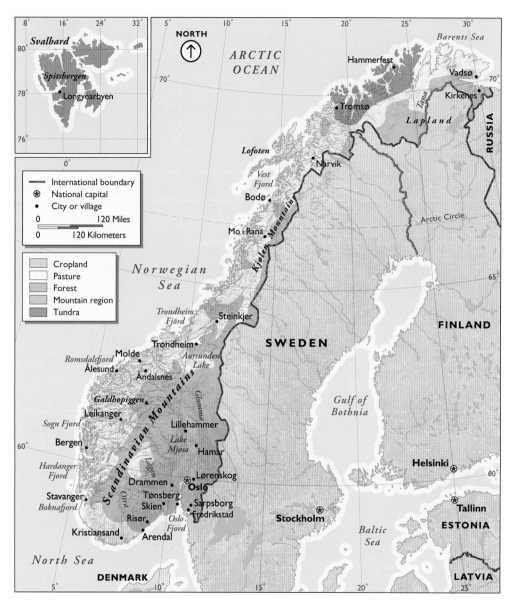

**Geography of Norway**

each year. In the far north, where the country narrows, mountains overlook the fjords and coastal islands. In the center and south, the mountains level out, forming high plateaus with permanent ice fields. The southeastern coast, from Oslo to Stavanger, is lowland. In all, two-thirds of Norway consists of tundra, rock, and snowfields, and another one-fourth is forested. Only approximately 3 percent—mostly in the southeast and in river valleys—is suitable for agriculture.[7]

## FJORDS

Norway's central west coast has some of the country's most spectacular fjords. Deep-blue ocean extends far into the interior. Steep cliffs surround the fjords, with isolated farms perched at the edges of forested ledges above. Each fjord has its own character and beauty. The country's longest fjord, Sogn Fjord, is 127 miles (204 km) long and 4,291 feet (1,308 m) deep.[10] Geirangerfjord and Nærøyfjord are listed as UNESCO World Heritage Sites. Both have spectacular waterfalls and breathtaking scenery, but increasing tourism is beginning to spoil the effect with noise and diesel fumes.

Its long, fjord-fringed coastline and many islands ensure that Norway and its people are strongly influenced by the sea, but Norway is also a land of freshwater. Its mountains are covered with glaciers and its valleys filled with lakes fed by glacial meltwater. The country has 7,537 square miles (19,520 sq km) of water in addition to its land area.[8] This includes more than 150,000 lakes.[9] The largest is Lake Mjøsa. Like most Norwegian lakes, it is long and thin, approximately 62 miles (100 km) long and ranging from one to nine miles (1.6 to 14 km) wide. Its deepest point is 1,473 feet (449 m).[11]

The country's major rivers include the Lågen, which flows into Lake Mjøsa in south-central Norway; the Tana River in the far north; and the Glomma, Norway's longest river. The Glomma runs for 372 miles (599 km) through Norway's forests.[12] Lumber companies float logs downstream on the Glomma to sawmills and paper mills in Sarpsborg. The river is also one of Norway's major sources of hydroelectric power.

## NORWAY'S CLIMATE

Because Norway is at the same latitude as Siberia, Greenland, and Alaska, one might expect a frigid climate. But the presence of the warm Gulf Stream current just off the western shore moderates winter temperatures, even above the Arctic Circle. The climate varies from

**The aurora borealis fills the sky with color over a fjord.**

north to south, with the north being much cooler and snowier. But even in the north, July temperatures may reach as high as 86 degrees Fahrenheit (30°C).[13] Climate also varies from east to west, partly because of the mountains. Bergen, on the Atlantic coast, has an average January temperature of 35 degrees Fahrenheit (1.6°C). Oslo, at about the same latitude but east of the mountains, averages 25 degrees Fahrenheit (−3.9°C) in January. Summer temperatures are warm, but not hot. The average July temperature in Bergen is 58 degrees Fahrenheit (14.5°C); in Oslo, it is 65 degrees Fahrenheit (18.3°C).[14]

The west coast is also wetter and often has strong winds. On average, Bergen has up to 80 inches (200 cm) of rain and more than

## AVERAGE TEMPERATURE AND PRECIPITATION

| Region (City) | Average January Temperature (Minimum/Maximum) | Average July Temperature (Minimum/Maximum) | Average Precipitation (January/July) |
|---|---|---|---|
| Southern Norway (Oslo) | 20/31°F (-7/-.5°C) | 55/71°F (13/22°C) | 1.9/3.2 inches (4.8/8.1 cm) |
| Southwestern Fjords (Bergen) | 30/38°F (-1/3°C) | 51/62°F (11/17°C) | 7.5/5.8 inches (19/14.7 cm) |
| Western Fjords (Ålesund) | 34/39°F (1/4°C) | 53/59°F (12/15°C) | 4.8/3.4 inches (12.2/8.6 cm) |
| Trøndelag (Trondheim) | 22/33°F (-6/.5°C) | 52/64°F (11/18°C) | 2.4/3.5 inches (6/8.9 cm) |
| Nordland (Mo i Rana) | 20/26°F (-7/-3°C) | 52/61°F (11/16°C) | 6.1/3.5 inches (15.5/8.9 cm)[16] |

200 rainy days per year. Some eastern and inland areas, protected from the coast by the central mountains, receive only approximately 12 inches (30 cm) of rain per year.[15]

**NORTH**

ARCTIC
OCEAN

*Barents Sea*

Hammerfest
Vadsø
Tromsø
Narvik
*Vest Fjord*
Bodø

*Norwegian Sea*

Steinkjer
*Trondheim Fjord*
Molde
Trondheim
*Romsdalsfjord*

*Gulf of Bothnia*

Leikanger
Lillehammer
*Sogn Fjord*
Bergen
Hamar
*Hardanger Fjord*
*Lågen*
Tønsberg
Oslo
Stavanger
Sarpsborg
*Oslo Fjord*
Kristiansand
Arendal

*North Sea*

*Baltic Sea*

Longyearbyen

| | |
|---|---|
| | Temperate, No Dry Season, Warm Summer |
| | Cold, Dry, Cold Summer |
| | Cold, No Dry Season, Warm Summer |
| | Cold, No Dry Season, Cold Summer |
| | Alpine or Polar Tundra |

**Climate of Norway**

# CHAPTER 3

# ANIMALS AND NATURE: NORTHERN DIVERSITY

The island of Svalbard, in the far North Arctic, does not look like an inviting animal habitat. More than half of its surface is ice, and less than 10 percent of the rest has vegetation.[1] But during the summer, Svalbard explodes with life. Whales and fish congregate offshore, seals and walruses feed in the ocean and breed onshore, and millions of seabirds raise young in precarious nests built on vertical cliffs. This teeming food web depends on rich blooms of plankton in springtime, fed by a branch of the warm Gulf Stream current, called the West Spitsbergen current, which swirls around the island's coastline. At the top of this food web are the island's 3,000 polar bears, which feed on seals. Inland, reindeer forage for the sparse vegetation and arctic foxes hunt birds and small mammals.

**A polar bear lounges on an ice block on Svalbard.**

**Norway is one of the few places in the world to view musk oxen in the wild.**

The rest of Norway, although not as diverse as warmer regions, has abundant wildlife and vegetation as well. A few species are found only in Norway or Scandinavia; others are typical of all northern regions. These plants and animals are spread throughout Norway's ecosystems: the frigid tundra in the far north and mountains; the temperate forested valleys and mountain slopes; and the many lakes and rivers, which teem with fish and other aquatic organisms.

## TUNDRA

The land above the Arctic Circle is Arctic tundra. The soil of this cold, desertlike region is permafrost from ten to 36 inches (25 to 90 cm) down.[2] Tundra is a treeless environment with coarse grasses, heather, thorny evergreen shrubs, hardy dwarf shrubs, wildflowers, mosses, and lichens. Yearly precipitation, including melting snow, is very low. The poorly drained soil forms bogs and ponds that provide moisture for plants. The growing seasons lasts approximately 60 days. Animals must either withstand or avoid the extreme temperatures. Typical herbivores include lemmings, voles, arctic hares, squirrels, and reindeer.

Small populations of musk oxen have been reintroduced into national parks in the tundra. Tundra carnivores include arctic foxes,

### SURVIVING THE TUNDRA

Year-round tundra dwellers have two basic strategies to get food for winter survival: they keep hunting, or they store energy. Polar bears (except pregnant ones) remain active all winter, capturing seals as they surface at breathing holes. But when seals are scarce, polar bears enter a state of walking hibernation in which their metabolism decreases. Reindeer, musk oxen, and rock ptarmigan store fat before winter. Reindeer fat stores may be four inches (10 cm) thick. Arctic foxes use both strategies. They continue hunting throughout the winter, and their coats turn white to provide camouflage. But they also dig dens in the side of a hill or cliff for shelter, and when hunting does not provide food, they eat food killed and stored earlier.

## ALPINE TUNDRA

Alpine tundra occurs in mountainous areas above the tree line. The growing season is longer than for Arctic tundra—approximately 180 days—and the soil is well drained. Vegetation is similar to that in the Arctic tundra. Mammals include pikas, marmots, mountain goats, sheep, and elk. There are also many grouse-like birds.

wolves, wolverines, and weasels. A substantial population of polar bears exists on Svalbard. The tundra also buzzes with insects, including mosquitoes, flies, moths, and grasshoppers. Migratory birds such as ravens, snow buntings, falcons, loons, sandpipers, and gulls descend on the region every summer.

Hundreds of thousands of seabirds—including terns, gannets, guillemots, puffins, kittiwakes, and skuas—nest on northern coasts and on offshore island cliffs.

## FORESTS

Several tiers of forests grow up the slopes and fill the valleys of Norway's mountains. Thick forests of Norway spruce and Scotch pine grow in the broad valleys. These regions are also home to deciduous trees including birch, alder, ash, rowan, and aspen. Forest floors are carpeted with leafy

**Puffins are one of the many species of seabird that nest on the north coasts and island cliffs of Norway.**

mosses and heathers, and wild blueberries, cranberries, and cloudberries are abundant. Cloudberries, found only in Scandinavia and Britain, are tart berries related to raspberries and blackberries and are much prized for use in desserts and preserves. Above this temperate zone is a zone of birch trees, and even higher is a zone supporting willows and dwarf birches. Elk roam the spruce-pine forests, and red deer abound in western forests. Foxes, otters, and martens are found in the east and southeast. Partridges and grouse, common in mountain forests, are popular game birds. Norway is also home to larger birds, including ospreys, eagles, and owls.

> Norway's national bird, the dipper, can stay underwater for up to 30 seconds.

## AQUATIC HABITATS

The most common freshwater fish are salmon, trout, grayling, perch, and pike. Trout and salmon are found in rivers and streams and attract sportfishing enthusiasts from around the world. Major coastal fish include herring, cod, mackerel, and halibut. Fishing (and more recently aquaculture) is a bedrock of Norway's coastal economy. The Gulf Stream provides abundant food for fish populations, and Norwegians have exploited this abundance by fishing without limits. Overfishing led to record fish catches in the 1960s, followed by crashes of both herring and cod populations. In 1977, the government established conservation

**Forests of snow-covered pine trees in Trysil, Norway**

## WHALING AND SEALING

In 1986, whale populations worldwide were seriously endangered due to unrestricted whaling. The International Whaling Commission (IWC) proposed a suspension of whaling to prevent extinctions. Norway, along with Japan and Iceland, refused to abide by the ban. Some Norwegians claim the ban is outdated, because today's whalers adhere to quotas, use more humane killing methods, and limit hunting to minke whales, which are not currently endangered. They do not plan to resume commercial whaling, only family operations. They see the ban as a threat to a traditional industry and their freedom of action.

practices, including offshore limits and quota agreements with other countries. In September 2011, they closed a large section of deep ocean to certain fishing methods, protecting an area of bottom habitat more than twice the size of mainland Norway.

Norwegian waters are filled with fish and marine mammals, including many whale species. Baleen whales are attracted by the rich plankton populations, and predators such as sperm whales are drawn by the fish and other sea mammals. Dolphins, seals, and walruses all have populations in the area. Many of the whale species are highly endangered, and there is little chance their populations will recover.

## ENVIRONMENTAL ISSUES

Norway has a reputation as an environmentally responsible country. Almost the entire country recycles, and the government strongly regulates industrial waste. Environmental problems are mostly related to the country's wealthy lifestyle and high technology. Air quality has improved since the 1990s but remains a problem in major cities. Air pollution from vehicle emissions, industries, and wood-burning stoves generates acid rain, which damages surrounding forests and lakes and threatens fish stocks.

Emissions also include greenhouse gases, which contribute to climate change and melting glaciers. During the last Ice Age, all of Norway was covered by glaciers; today, glaciers cover only approximately 1 percent of the mainland. Some interior glaciers shrank by as much as one and one-half miles (2.5 km) during the twentieth century, and their ice is also thinning rapidly.[3] Melting glaciers

**Orcas can be seen in Vest Fjord off the northwestern coast of Norway.**

threaten Norway's power supply, since 15 percent of Norway's electricity comes from hydropower plants on glacier-fed rivers.[4] The tourism industry, too, will suffer if glaciers disappear. Much of human-caused climate change is due to greenhouse gas release from burning fossil fuels. Even though Norway's use of fossil fuels is very low, Norwegians contribute significantly to this global problem through their large exports of oil and gas. Norwegians try to compensate for their contribution to climate change by working actively for international climate-control efforts and pledging to reduce their own greenhouse gas production.

## THREATENED SPECIES

Compared to many countries, Norway still has considerable pristine wilderness. But some habitats, such as peat bogs, river deltas, deciduous forests, and sand dunes, are now considered endangered. Norway's Nature Diversity Act, passed in 2009, protects approximately 17 percent of Norway's mainland, mostly mountainous areas.[5] It provides new rules and tools for identifying and protecting endangered habitats. It is designed to work with other statutes regulating use of the natural environment, including those relating to land use for transportation, energy, and construction as well as natural

**The Svalbard Archipelago has more polar bears than people.**

**The lynx is one of Norway's threatened species.**

## ENDANGERED SPECIES IN NORWAY

According to the International Union for Conservation of Nature (IUCN), Norway is home to the following numbers of species that are categorized by the organization as Critically Endangered, Endangered, or Vulnerable:

| | |
|---|---|
| Mammals | 7 |
| Birds | 2 |
| Reptiles | 0 |
| Amphibians | 0 |
| Fishes | 19 |
| Mollusks | 4 |
| Other Invertebrates | 6 |
| Fungi | -- |
| Plants | 4 |
| Total | 42[6] |

resource use in fisheries, hunting, and forestry.

Areas protected under the Nature Diversity Act include nature reserves, national parks, and a few other areas. Norway has 42 national parks, including 35 on the mainland and seven on Svalbard. Almost 85 percent of the parks are in mountainous areas. The parks provide vast undisturbed spaces for animals such as wild reindeer, predators, and birds of prey, which may be threatened by contact with humans. Wild areas of Svalbard have been protected since the 1925 Svalbard Act, which was updated in 2002. Approximately 65 percent of the island is protected, as well as 75 percent of the surrounding territorial waters.[7]

Loss of wilderness is mainly due to agriculture and forestry. In addition, hydropower dams, tourism, pollution, and climate change are causing serious problems. As habitats are destroyed or fragmented, species struggle to survive. Threatened animals include wild reindeer, arctic foxes, bears, wolves, wolverines, lynx, and Atlantic salmon. Marine environments face threats as well, as exemplified by a serious oil spill that happened near the city of Langesund on July 31, 2009.

## SVALBARD GLOBAL SEED VAULT

The Svalbard Global Seed Vault, opened in 2008, is a cavern big enough to hold 4 million different types of seeds (a total of 2.25 billion seeds). Called the "vegetarian Noah's ark" or the "Doomsday Vault," its purpose is to preserve Earth's plant diversity. If a plant goes extinct, but its seeds have been saved in the vault, the plant can be brought back from extinction. The vault is built into the side of a mountain, under permafrost but 427 feet (130 m) above sea level so it will be protected from future sea level rises. Seeds are kept at a constant 0 degrees Fahrenheit (-18°C). Svalbard was considered safe because of its permafrost and because it is free from earthquakes and volcanoes. As of 2010, the vault protected 250 million seeds from 500,000 species.[8]

# CHAPTER 4

# HISTORY: ROAD TO PROSPERITY

At the end of the last Ice Age, approximately 10,000 years ago, the ancestors of the Sami people, who still live in Norway today, began moving into the region. Some traveled from Siberia in the east; others came up from the south. Eventually all of present-day Norway, Sweden, Finland, and the Kola Peninsula of Russia were inhabited. Some tribes settled near the sea and became dependent on fishing. Inland tribes became hunter-gatherers and fished the lakes. Far northern groups herded reindeer. Farming began in approximately 3,000 BCE. When the Iron Age started in approximately 500 BCE, people began building larger ships and clearing farmland.

**The Rock Art of Alta is the earliest rock art listed by the UNESCO World Heritage Centre.**

**The Rock Art of Alta, dated to approximately 4200 to 500 BCE, offers clues about human activity in the Far North during the prehistoric period.**

# THE VIKINGS

From approximately 800 CE to 1066 CE, Vikings dominated the region now called Norway. Historians have been unable to pinpoint the ancestors of the Vikings. They probably descended from three tribes that moved up from the south, although evidence also exists for central Asian ancestry. The Vikings were expert shipbuilders and seafarers. The Viking age officially began in 793 CE when Vikings attacked the Lindisfarne monastery off the coast of England. Norwegian Vikings raided the coasts of England, Scotland, and Ireland, and later Greenland and Iceland. They attacked, murdered, and terrorized coastal populations, displacing many of the people. But they also traded and formed settlements in these areas, as well as in northern islands such as the Orkneys and Hebrides. Over the

## VIKING SHIPS

Vikings built merchant ships and warships. Merchant ships were partly enclosed, to carry cargo, and were powered mostly by sail. Warships were longer, narrower, and shallower. They were completely open, powered by oars or sail, and built to be fast and maneuverable. Typical warships had approximately 16 rowers per side, but important ones, such as the king's flagship, had 30 or more rowers per side. Because their keels were not far below the waterline, warships could be maneuvered far up narrow rivers or easily landed on sand or gravel beaches. This made raids easier and more efficient.

**A replica of a Viking ship is anchored at a harbor in the Lofoten Islands.**

years, the Vikings transformed Scandinavia into a world power. They traded fish and furs for spices, metals, ceramics, glass, and other goods. They also brought back technology and slaves, increasing the Norwegian standard of living. Vikings formed a merchant class and many left to settle the coasts of conquered countries. Norwegian farmers emigrated to settle Iceland, Greenland, and the Faroe Islands.

As Viking chieftains conquered foreign lands, they also warred among themselves. In approximately 890, Harald I defeated his fellow chieftains and united the tribes under a single government for the first time in Norway's history. Thus, Harald was Norway's first king, but his united government lasted only until his death. In 995, Harald's descendant Olaf I Tryggvason tried unsuccessfully to Christianize Norway by force. But Queen Sigrid of Sweden, his intended wife, refused to convert and instead married Svein Forkbeard of Denmark, the Danish king. The pair worked together to

## SAINT OLAF

Olaf II Haraldsson spent most of his life abroad, where he converted to Christianity. He returned to Norway in 1015 and united the country for the first time since the days of his ancestor, Harald I. He imposed Christianity as the state religion, using force when necessary. In 1028, King Knut of Denmark and England invaded, forcing Olaf to flee to Russia. He returned in 1030 but fell at the Battle of Stiklestad, near Nidaros (now Trondheim). The Nidaros Cathedral is said to have been built on or near his remains. He is now known as Saint Olaf, Norway's patron saint.

defeat and kill Olaf I. In 1015, King Olaf II Haraldsson returned from England, founded Norway's first national government, and forcibly imposed Christianity on the Norwegian people. He founded the Church of Norway in 1024. Olaf II was overthrown by the Danes at the Battle of Stiklestad in 1030. He was later canonized as Saint Olaf and is considered Norway's patron saint. As Christianity rose, Viking rule declined. A raid on England by King Harald III Sigurdsson in 1066 ended in the king's defeat and death, and Viking warriors quickly faded into history.

## GAIN AND LOSS OF INDEPENDENCE

During the Middle Ages, Norway's population grew, farming expanded, and civil wars were fought over succession to the throne. During this Norwegian "period of greatness" from 1217 to 1319, many churches and other buildings were constructed, including the Nidaros Cathedral in Trondheim and the Akershus Fortress in Oslo. At the end of this period, Norway reached a high point in population. In 1319, King Magnus I, grandson of Norway's King Haakon V, united Sweden and Norway. This began approximately 200 years of decline, in which populations fell and Norway became part of a Scandinavian state that changed hands several times. A major cause of the decline was bubonic plague, or the Black Death, which swept through Europe and up the coast of Norway in 1349. The plague killed two-thirds of the Norwegian

**The Norwegian language has no word for city.**

population and 80 percent of its nobility.[1] Outbreaks of plague continued until approximately 1500. Farms, governments, towns, and trade declined. Surviving members of the nobility were forced to leave their once-wealthy lifestyles and become farmers again. This was the beginning of the egalitarian society that Norway maintains to the present day.

In 1397, the Kalmar Union was formed, uniting Sweden, Denmark, and Norway into a single country. Sweden left the union in 1523, but Denmark retained control over Norway. In 1537, in the wake of the Protestant Reformation, Denmark forced Norway to convert from a Catholic to a Lutheran country. The Danish king became head of the church and the largest Norwegian landowner. Danish nobility held offices in Norway, and the Norwegian written language disappeared,

## BLACK DEATH

Bubonic plague is carried by rodents and transmitted to people by rodents' fleas. The infection spreads and kills very quickly. It causes fever and painful swellings of the lymph nodes, plus black spots on the skin. In the 1330s, a plague outbreak in China was spread to Europe on Chinese trading ships. Within five years, one-third of the European population had died. Plague is caused by a bacterium, *Yersinia pestis*, and today doctors can treat it with antibiotics.

**The Nidaros Cathedral in Trondheim, built between the twelfth and fourteenth centuries, has been damaged and rebuilt several times.**

although spoken dialects continued. For several hundred years, Norwegians were subjected to Danish rule, poor living conditions, and ongoing wars between Denmark and other European countries.

During the Napoleonic Wars, from approximately 1803 to 1815, Denmark allied itself with France, and when France was defeated, the Danes surrendered. As part of their surrender, they transferred Norway to Sweden in compensation for Sweden's loss of Finland to Russia. On January 14, 1814, under pressure from Sweden, Norway signed the Treaty of Kiel, becoming part of Sweden in what was called the Union of the Crowns. Unhappy about being passed from one ruler to another, some Norwegians rebelled. They wrote their own constitution and elected a king, Prince Christian Frederik of Denmark. The Constitution was accepted on May 17, 1814, but the new Norwegian king was soon forced to give up the throne. A compromise was reached in which Sweden recognized the Norwegian constitution and parliament but still retained veto power over Norway's actions and controlled foreign policy.

**Dutch explorer Willem Barents discovered the Svalbard Archipelago in 1596.**

**A woman in a horse-drawn carriage on the road to Stalheim, Norway, circa 1890**

# INDEPENDENT NORWAY

During the nineteenth century, Norway began rebuilding its confidence and underwent a cultural revival in an effort to define its national identity. This century produced some of Norway's greatest artists, musicians, and writers, including playwright Henrik Ibsen, painter Edvard Munch, and composer Edvard Grieg. Two standardized written Norwegian languages were developed simultaneously. One, called Riksmål (later Bokmål) was Norwegianized Danish. The other, Landsmål, or Nynorsk, was developed from Norwegian dialects. The country began developing the infrastructure and economic base for future growth, completing its first railroad in 1854 and expanding its fishing and whaling industries. However, Norway remained very poor, and from 1825 to 1925, more than 750,000 Norwegians emigrated to the United States and Canada.[2]

On June 7, 1905, Norway's parliament voted against continued union with Sweden, which had been in force since the 1814 Treaty of Kiel. The Norwegian people confirmed their support of the parliament's vote, and on October 26, 1905, the Swedish king, Oskar II, abdicated his control of Norway. He was replaced by Danish Prince Carl, who was chosen by the Norwegian parliament to be King Haakon VII of Norway. Norway officially became an independent constitutional monarchy.

Buoyed by its new independence, Norway set about proving its worth to the international community. It began developing hydroelectric

**King Haakon VII, pictured with Queen Maud and Prince Olaf, became the first king of Norway when the country gained its independence in 1905.**

power, making it easier to harness the country's natural resources. Industry developed rapidly, and Norway quickly became an export economy. In 1913, it became one of the first European countries to give women the vote, ushering in a strong tradition of gender equality. The country remained neutral during World War I (1914–1918), and its industries and exports—particularly shipping, mining, and fishing— flourished. However, approximately half of the Norwegian shipping fleet was sunk by German submarines.[3] In the 1920s, Norway acquired the Jan Mayen and Svalbard Islands. Economic expansion continued, and the country's industrial production increased by 75 percent between 1913 and 1938.[4] Even so, the depression of the 1920s and 1930s hit Norway hard. By 1933, one-third of the workforce was unemployed.[5]

## NORWAY AND WORLD WAR II

In 1933, former defense minister Vidkun Quisling formed a Norwegian Fascist Party, which lost favor as it became increasingly allied with the German Nazis. As World War II (1939–1945) broke out in Europe, Norway again declared its neutrality, but it could not hold out as fascism overtook Europe. On April 9, 1940, the Germans invaded Norway. Quisling announced the invasion on a live radio broadcast and appointed himself head of a new ad-hoc government, expecting German support. But he was replaced by German Josef Terboven five days later. Terboven,

**Oslo residents line the sidewalks as German troops move through the town on May 2, 1940.**

as commissioner, reported directly to Adolf Hitler, but kept Quisling on as minister president, hoping to decrease Norwegians' resentment of the takeover. This did not succeed. But even with help from Allied forces, the Norwegian Army could not stem the invasion. The royal family went into exile, and Norwegian troops capitulated on June 10.

But Norwegians were not about to surrender to German occupation. In five years of war, Norway built up a resistance movement of 40,000 people and 60 underground newspapers.[6] Although many were arrested, the Norwegian resistance became well known for sabotage. Their destruction of the Germans' heavy water plant at Vemork helped foil Germany's attempts to build an atomic bomb.

Norway suffered for its resistance. Six towns were burned in the initial invasion. The Germans imposed martial law and executed resistance members who were caught. They sent 770 Norwegian Jews to the Auschwitz concentration camp in Poland and imprisoned another 50 in Norway. Approximately 930 Jews escaped to Sweden.[7] When the Germans were forced from Norway in late 1944 and early 1945, they burned and devastated Finnmark and northern Troms as they retreated. Quisling and 24 other collaborators were tried and executed shortly after the Germans surrendered.

**In 1942 Oslo, a queue forms early in the morning outside a shop as people get in line hoping to buy food from limited supplies.**

# MODERN NORWAY

After the war, Norway directed its efforts toward rebuilding production capacity, housing, and infrastructure rather than producing consumer goods. The country recovered quickly, partly with assistance from the European Recovery Program, also known as the Marshall Plan. Norway remained involved internationally when it became a founding member of the United Nations in 1945. The majority party between 1945 and 1965 was the Norwegian Labour Party, which continued and expanded social programs begun in the 1930s. These included universal old-age pensions, a compulsory earnings-related supplementary pension plan, and a national welfare assistance law. Norway's standard of living rose rapidly, and there was almost full employment until the 1980s.

## THE MARSHALL PLAN

The European Recovery Plan (later called the Marshall Plan) was proposed by US Secretary of State George C. Marshall. Between 1948 and 1952, the plan provided $13 billion to help rebuild European countries devastated by the war. Norway used its share ($256 million) to rebuild housing and infrastructure, including hydroelectric dams, and to rebuild industries such as fishing, canning, and cruise ships.[8] As other European economies recovered, they also improved Norway's economy by importing Norwegian products.

In 1969, petroleum and natural gas deposits were discovered in the North Sea off Norway's coast, and the oil industry quickly dominated

**Norwegian right-wing leader Vidkun Quisling,** *left*, **meets with Adolf Hitler in January 1945.**

Norway's economy. Oil revenues have made Norway one of the richest countries in the world. The government has been very responsible in using its oil revenues. It began by paying off its national debt, and then began reinvesting profits in the Norwegian Government Pension Fund Global, which will be used to maintain its social programs, such as

government pensions and health care.

Norway's oil wealth continues to grow. Since 1970, the country has had a succession of mostly socialist governments and has developed one of the most complete social welfare systems in the world. Citizens are entitled to free medical care, higher education, pensions, and unemployment benefits. Its government claims to be "the most egalitarian social democracy in Western Europe."[9] Despite its small size and population, Norway is well known in international circles as an advocate for peace and democracy. However, the nation has steadfastly retained its independence, cooperating with other European countries but refusing twice to join the European Union.

## NORWAY'S EXPLORERS

Norwegian explorers such as Fridtjof Nansen (1861–1930) and Roald Amundsen (1872–1928) have continued the Viking tradition of exploration. In 1888, Nansen headed a six-man expedition to Greenland, where he studied and later authored a book on the Inuit. In 1893, he spent several years exploring the Arctic and made a failed attempt to reach the North Pole. Roald Amundsen, in 1897, was part of the first expedition to overwinter in the Antarctic. From 1903 to 1905, he led an expedition that became the first to navigate the Northwest Passage. On December 14, 1911, Amundsen and three companions became the first men to reach the South Pole, beating explorer Robert Falcon Scott by one month and three days. Amundsen disappeared in May 1928 while on a rescue mission in the Arctic.

**In 2005, the royal family paraded through Oslo on its way to a ceremony marking the one hundredth anniversary of Norway's independence.**

# CHAPTER 5

# PEOPLE: VIKING ROOTS

Norway has low racial and ethnic diversity, although that is rapidly changing. As of 2007, more than 94 percent of the population was Norwegian.[1] By January 2012, this had decreased to 86.9 percent due to increasing immigration.[2] Traditionally, Norwegians have been known for their tall, blond, Viking appearance. The largest minority group is the indigenous Sami. Five other minority groups have official status: the Kvens, Forest Finns, Romani (originally from India), Roma (gypsies), and Jews. All have suffered some persecution, but all now have organizations dedicated to their needs and are covered in public schools' curriculum. The groups are very small. Some, such as the Forest Finns, are assimilated into Norwegian society.

Until recently, most immigrants to Norway have been Europeans, many from Germany, Denmark, Sweden, and Finland. A few Jews migrated

**Many Norwegians still dress in traditional costumes for festivals.**

to Norway in the late nineteenth century; more arrived as refugees from Nazism in the 1930s. In 1975, new restrictions were placed on immigration. But, with a long-lived and aging population, the country had labor shortages and a growing need for skilled workers. In the 1990s, Norway made it easier for highly skilled workers to enter the country to seek employment. Other foreigners enter the country to seek asylum or to reunite with their families. Immigration from outside Europe is expected to increase greatly in the coming years.

The influx of immigrants with different attitudes and values has stressed Norwegian society. The largest groups come from Poland, Sweden, and Germany, but more than half are from non-Western countries—principally Pakistan, Somalia, Iraq, Iran, Bosnia, and Kosovo. Most Norwegians feel the immigrants' cultural and racial differences enrich Norway's culture, and they believe immigrants are entitled to the same opportunities as native citizens. But others blame immigration for increasing crime rates and resent newcomers for taking advantage of the welfare system.

## THE SAMI TODAY

The Sami are indigenous to Norway, Sweden, Finland, and Russia. The largest population, at approximately 40,000, lives in Norway.[3] They are descended from the hunter-gatherers who arrived very early in Norwegian

**Pedestrians travel a street in Bergen that is lined with shops and cafés.**

history, probably from Siberia, and spent thousands of years as wild reindeer herders. Reindeer herding is still a major part of their economy. Throughout the nineteenth and part of the twentieth centuries, the Norwegian government considered the Sami to be at a lower social level from other Norwegians. Norway attempted to assimilate the Sami into modern culture by educating them in the same way as other Norwegian children. This was considered the best way to promote equality between Sami and other Norwegians. Unfortunately, in doing so, they removed the children from all exposure to Sami culture and language.

Beginning in the 1960s, the Sami people became much more assertive and political. In 1989, they formed the Sami Parliament, which elects representatives from all over Norway and acts to preserve Sami language and culture. Currently Norway has Sami schools, businesses, social organizations, and political parties. Land claims and hunting rights are still under discussion, but the Sami now actively work for an equal place in Norwegian society and help promote indigenous rights internationally.

## LANGUAGE

During the four centuries of Danish rule, Norway's official language was Danish. Official Norwegian written languages were developed in the nineteenth century, as Norway began creating its own national identity.

**A Sami family wearing traditional Sami costumes makes its home near Kjøllefjord.**

## YOU SAY IT!

| English | Norwegian |
|---|---|
| Hello (good day) | God dag (goo DAHG) |
| Good-bye | Ha det (HAH deh) |
| Please | Vær så snill (vah shuh SNILL) |
| Thank you | Takk (TAHKK) |
| Yes | Ja (YAH) |
| No | Nei (NAHEE) |
| Excuse me | Unnskyld (OON-shul) |
| Sorry | Beklager (Bay-KLAH-gehr) |
| Do you speak English? | Snakker du engelsk? (SNAH-ker doo EHNG-ehlsk?) |
| What's your name? | Hva heter du? (vah HAY-ter doo?) |
| My name is | Jeg heter (yeh HAY-ter) |

The two written forms of Norwegian—Bokmål and Nynorsk—are similar enough to be mutually understood. Bokmål is derived from Danish. Nynorsk is a compilation of dialects from throughout Norway, and informed by Old Norse. Each school chooses one language to teach young children, but by eighth grade, students must learn both. Sami is also an official language in six municipalities.

## RELIGION

Norway has been mostly homogeneous with respect to religion as well as ethnicity. In January 2010, 79.2 percent of Norwegians belonged to the Evangelical Lutheran Church of Norway, which was the state church from 1814 to 2012.[4] Since 1964, freedom of religion has been guaranteed by the constitution in Norway.

**NORWAY'S RELIGIOUS GROUPS[5]**

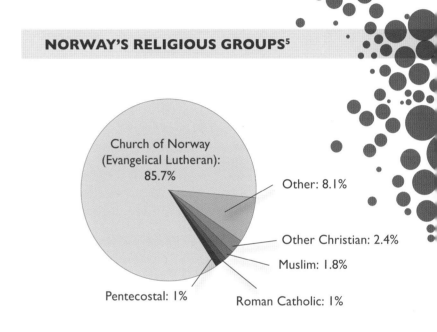

Church of Norway (Evangelical Lutheran): 85.7%

Other: 8.1%

Other Christian: 2.4%

Muslim: 1.8%

Pentecostal: 1%

Roman Catholic: 1%

## NORWAY'S CHILDBIRTH AND ADOPTION BENEFITS

Norway provides excellent benefits for new parents. Mothers are entitled to a six-week paid maternity leave plus three weeks of leave prior to childbirth. This can be extended to 47 weeks with full pay or 57 weeks with 80 percent pay, if desired. Fathers can also take a 12-week paternity leave as part of the family's 46 or 56 weeks. Except for the nine weeks reserved for the mother and the 12 weeks reserved for the father, the rest of the time may be divided between the parents as they wish. Each parent may also choose to take another full year of unpaid leave or up to two years of part-time work at full-time pay. For adoption, a family is entitled to the same leave, less the three weeks allowed prior to childbirth.[9]

All registered churches and philosophical societies receive tax funds. As of May 21, 2012, based on a parliamentary vote, the Church of Norway is no longer the state church and Norway is now a secular state. This means the state no longer has control over the church and cannot appoint bishops and pastors. Also, from now on, all other religions existing within Norway will be considered equal to the Church of Norway.

Overall, the country is becoming more secular. Approximately 2 percent of Norwegians attend church regularly, and traditional religious practices are declining.[6] Approximately 5,000 people per year are leaving the Church of Norway, although many still depend on it for important life passages, including funerals, baptisms, confirmations, and marriages.[7] Immigrants are also changing the face of religion in Norway. Twenty percent of religious people who are not members of the Church of Norway are Muslim.[8]

With a long-standing tradition of gender equality, Norway's women grow up with similar opportunities to Norwegian men.

## CHILDBIRTH AND GENDER EQUALITY

Most families in Norway have two children. The fertility rate, or number of children per female, averages 1.77, one of the highest in Europe.[10] This is probably due to the high level of support given to families. In 2010, the organization Save the Children ranked Norway "the best country in the world in which to have children," and the United Nations in 2009 ranked it the best place to be a woman.[11] Benefits for new parents are very generous, and families have few worries about money, jobs, or child care.

## GAY RIGHTS

From 1993 until 2009, same-sex couples in Norway could enter a registered partnership, or civil union, which took place before a notary public and within Norway. Civil unions did not include the right to adopt or undergo artificial insemination. On January 1, 2009, a new law went into effect that extended full marriage rights, including the right to adopt and to undergo artificial insemination, to same-sex couples. The new law gives clergy and individual congregations of the Church of Norway the right, but not the obligation, to perform gay marriages.

Norway has a long tradition of gender equality. Women received the right to vote on June 11, 1913. Laws were passed in 1918 and 1927 giving women equal status with men in areas of divorce, child custody, and property rights. The Gender Equality Act of 1978 mandated gender equality in the public sector, and a 2002 amendment extended it to the private sector. The United Nations ranks Norway second in the world for gender equality, based on factors such as number of female legislators and professional and technical workers, life expectancy, adult literacy rate, and earned income.

In general, Norway's population looks similar to that of many highly developed Western countries. It is relatively wealthy, with excellent health care, educational systems, and longevity. More so than many countries, Norwegians place a high priority on human rights and on ensuring all citizens have free and equal participation in society and equal access to its benefits.

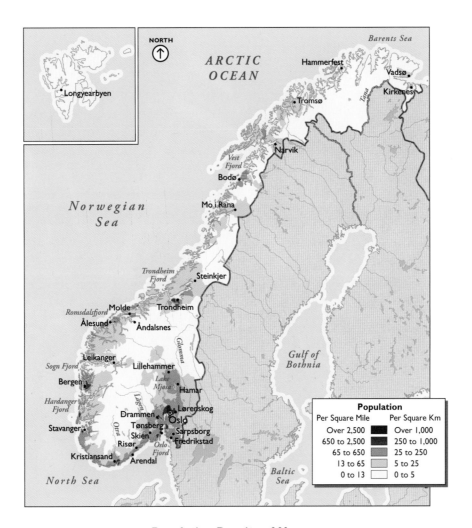

**Population Density of Norway**

Population

| Per Square Mile | Per Square Km |
|---|---|
| Over 2,500 | Over 1,000 |
| 650 to 2,500 | 250 to 1,000 |
| 65 to 650 | 25 to 250 |
| 13 to 65 | 5 to 25 |
| 0 to 13 | 0 to 5 |

# CHAPTER 6
# CULTURE: FOLK HERITAGE

Every May 17, Syttende mai, or Constitution Day, celebrations are in full swing in Norway. Whole towns turn out for parades of schoolchildren, teachers, and school bands. Schools organize and lead the parades and provide refreshments and entertainment. Later, families gather for a holiday meal. Many Norwegians wear *bunad*, or the traditional folk costume, which varies by region. Women and girls wear an embroidered wool skirt, waistcoat, and white shirt, sometimes with a cap or shawl. Men and boys wear a shirt and fitted black jacket with trousers and socks. *Russ*, or students about to graduate from high school, dress in baggy overalls and tasseled caps, which they are not allowed to take off until graduation day. The Norwegian flag flies everywhere. This celebration honors the day in 1814 on which the Constitution was signed, but it is very much a children's celebration.

**Children participate in the Constitution Day Children's Parade in Oslo.**

## HOLIDAYS AND FESTIVALS

Constitution Day is one of Norway's 22 official flag days and holidays per year. Some are religious, such as Christmas and Easter; others are political or patriotic, such as Workers Day and Constitution Day. On New Year's, Norwegians have fireworks and listen to speeches—the king speaks on New Year's Eve and the prime minister on New Year's Day. Saint John's Eve (June 23) celebrates the birth of John the Baptist, but it has become a secular holiday celebrated with huge bonfires, music, dancing, and food grilled outdoors.

A major celebration around the country is the Saint Olaf Festival, held during the week of July 29. In Trondheim, where Saint Olaf fell in battle, the festival includes a medieval market and lots of music—classical, pop, folk, and jazz—with big-name musicians from around the world. Stiklestad holds a similar festival, including Vikings in costume. During the last five days, an outdoor pageant recreates the conflicts between King Olaf, chieftains, and farmers. The huge cast includes Norway's top actors in major roles and locals in minor roles and as extras.

Other celebrations of Norway's colorful history and culture occur throughout the country. In early February, Tromsø celebrates Sami Week, highlighted by the national reindeer sledge championship. In June, the Viking Festival on Karmøy Island in the southwest features Viking feasts, processions, and evenings of sagas. Also in June, the Middle Ages festival, featuring period costumes and Gregorian chants in the glass cathedral, takes over the town of Hamar.

Traditional folk musicians perform at the
Norwegian Folk Museum.

## MUSIC AND DANCE

Norway has a long tradition of folk music. During the nineteenth century,
scholars, including Norway's greatest composer, Edvard Grieg, traveled
throughout the countryside listening to and writing down the music
for the first time. Much folk music was vocal. Work songs entertained
herders and helped call in their cattle or goats, or—in the case of sea

chanteys—gave rhythm to the work on sailing vessels. Herders made small horns and flutes, playing to pass the time as they watched their herds. Stringed instruments were used both for listening and dancing.

A uniquely Norwegian song form is the stev, a four-line song used in competitions or as a ballad refrain. Sometimes stevs were strung together to make longer songs. Ballads mostly revolved around heroic figures or the supernatural, including trolls and giants. Norway's most famous ballad, the "Draumkvedet," or "Dream Ballad," may date back to the thirteenth century. It is considered a national treasure in Norway and is often played today.

**Rikard Nordraak, who composed Norway's national song, died at age 23.**

Edvard Grieg is by far Norway's best-known composer. He used Norwegian folk music in his compositions and tried to develop a unique, identifiable Norwegian music. He wrote works for piano, orchestra, solo voice, and choir. His works include the *Piano Concerto in A Minor* and the *Peer Gynt Suites*. Grieg also collected and arranged Norwegian folk songs and set to music many poems, including some by the Danish fairy tale author Hans Christian Andersen.

In recent times Norway has produced many successful musicians and bands, but those who wish to become known internationally record in English. A highly successful international pop-rock band was the group A-ha, founded in 1985. Its hit single "Take on Me" remained on the US *Billboard* Hot 100 for 23 weeks, and its music video won six MTV awards in 1986.[1] It is the only Norwegian band to achieve such success. The band split up in 2010. One recent success has been the band Datarock, founded in 2000, which has had its songs featured in Coca-Cola and iPod commercials. The most successful Norwegian export in contemporary pop music is so-called black metal. It was made popular by the bands Mayhem, formed in 1984, and Turbonegro, formed in 1988.

## SPORTS AND LEISURE ACTIVITIES

Norwegians tend to be physically active and often participate in outdoor sports or join gyms or sports-oriented clubs—including archery, rifle shooting, skiing, and soccer. Most children participate in sports. Soccer, handball, and volleyball are popular in schools, and most areas have excellent sports facilities.

The country's love of winter sports is evident in events such as the Holmenkollen Ski Marathon near Oslo. This 34.8-mile (56 km) race runs through the Nordmarka forest to the Holmenkollen arena. In 2011, the marathon attracted more than 5,000 participants.[2] Also, the Finnmarksløpet, the world's second-longest and northernmost dogsled race tracks 621.4 miles (1,000 km) across northern Norway from Alta to Kirkenes and back again. The race runs for approximately six days in early March. In 2012, it was won by Inger-Marie Haaland, whose dogs beat 51 other teams.[3]

Norwegians cherish their country's beauty and appreciate the peace and calm associated with being in nature. They enjoy outdoor activities any time of year—including hiking, cross-country skiing, boating, fishing,

and hunting. Whenever possible, people leave the cities and head for the country. Approximately one-fourth of Norwegians own a *hytte*, or country cabin, where they spend weekends and holidays. Much of their time is spent walking or hiking in nature. Norwegian law gives people the right to roam through the countryside, even over other people's land, as long as they remain a certain distance from homes.

Norway has hosted the Winter Olympics twice, in Oslo in 1952 and in Lillehammer in 1994. The country has participated in nearly every Olympic Games since 1900, and it is a matter of pride for Norwegians to take home the most medals in the Winter Games. It achieved this goal in 1994 at Lillehammer

## BORN WITH SKIS ON

Norwegians' ancestors were traveling on skis at least 4,000 years ago. Virtually all Norwegians learn cross-country skiing and use this skill to traverse Norway's thousands of miles of trails and frozen lakes during the winter. Approximately 100 years ago, skiing became not just transportation, but a sport. Today, slalom, or downhill or alpine skiing, ranks as a top sport, along with snowboarding. Norway has produced more Winter Olympic medal winners than any other country. In 1998, cross-country skier Bjørn Dæhli became the most successful Winter Olympic athlete in history when he won his eighth gold medal. Norway's athletes have also excelled in figure skating and speed skating. Other Olympic stars from Norway include figure skater Sonja Henie, who won gold medals in 1928, 1932, and 1936, and speed skater Johann Koss, who won three gold medals in 1994.

**Norwegians enjoy outdoor winter sports such as cross-country skiing.**

A busy fish market in Bergen, Norway

and in 2002, and it came in second in 1998. But to the country's consternation, it has lost ground in recent Olympics, finishing thirteenth in 2006 and fourth in 2010.[4]

## FOOD

Norway's traditional foods include grains and fish. Barley and rye have been used since Viking times. Rice and potatoes were imported in the eighteenth and nineteenth centuries and quickly took hold. Rice porridge with butter and cinnamon is still a Christmas tradition. Fish has always been a staple food, and people quickly learned ways to preserve it. Often it was dried on rocks or specially built racks. Lutefisk, perhaps the best-known traditional Norwegian food, is dried codfish that has been soaked in a lye solution for several days before cooking. Most of today's fish are preserved by more modern methods. Similar to many other cultures, Norwegians now eat canned sardines and mackerel, pickled herring, smoked salmon, and frozen fish of various kinds.

## LITERATURE

Norway's earliest literature was oral poetry composed in Old Norse that originated in Iceland, where Norwegians settled in the ninth century. Much of it was about Norse heroes and gods. In approximately 1050, when Christianity reached Norway, the Latin language was introduced. The first forms of literature were religious texts and some legal texts. In the thirteenth century, literate people began writing down the oral poetry of Iceland, as well as prose stories, or sagas, about Norwegian kings, families, and legends. The most famous of these, from the fourteenth century, was *Heimskringla*, a king's saga by Icelandic historian Snorri Sturluson. Almost no Norwegian literature was written for approximately 200 years following the Black Plague because not many literate people survived.

Beginning in the sixteenth century, when Norway's Danish rulers replaced Catholicism with Lutheranism, Norwegians had to change to the Danish language. Throughout this century and much of the

## NORSE MYTHOLOGY

Norse mythology, the legends told by the Vikings of Scandinavia, weaves complex tales filled with many gods and goddesses. The Norse gods were divided into two major groups, the Vanir and the Aesir. The Vanir were peaceful gods and goddesses of fertility or production. They included Njord, his son, Freyr, and his daughter, Freyja. The later, more warlike Aesir gods did not destroy the Vanir, but reached an agreement in which the two groups had equal status and were able to intermarry. Odin, leader of the Aesir and the wisest god, had two ravens that kept him informed of the activities of gods, humans, giants, and dwarves. He was a seeker of knowledge who often changed into a human. Thor, son of Odin, was the god of thunder. He is known for possessing three rare objects—a mighty hammer, a belt of strength, and iron gloves.

seventeenth century, most literature was religious. Dorothe Engelbretsdotter (1634–1716), a popular poet, wrote Baroque hymns. Another important writer of this time, Petter Dass (1647–1707), wrote poetry, but he is most famous for his *Nordlands Trompet* (*The Trumpet of Nordland*), describing the life and geography of the northern Norwegian coast. Later in the eighteenth century, Ludvig Holberg (1684–1754) wrote poetry, plays, novels, essays, and philosophical works. Best known as a playwright, he is considered the father of both Norwegian and Danish literature and theater.

The romantic period in the nineteenth century was ushered in by authors Henrik Wergeland, Johan Sebastian Welhaven, and Camilla Collett. This gave way in the latter half of the century to the "Four

**A statue of Henrik Ibsen stands outside the National Theatre in Oslo.**

Greats" of Norwegian literature: Henrik Ibsen, Bjørnstjerne Bjørnson, Jonas Lie, and Alexander Kielland. Of these, playwright Ibsen is by far the best known internationally, especially for plays dealing with controversial topics.

Twentieth-century writers followed a tradition of realism, writing about individuals struggling in society. Their works dealt with politics,

## HENRIK IBSEN

Henrik Ibsen (1828–1906) was Norway's greatest playwright. He began writing plays as an in-house director for theaters in Bergen and Oslo, which was called Christiania at the time. In 1864, he moved with his wife and son to Italy and spent the next 27 years abroad. His breakthrough plays were *Brand* (1866) and *Peer Gynt* (1867). After meeting Danish intellectual Georg Brandes, Ibsen began writing dramas criticizing hypocrisy and corruption in society. His play *A Doll's House* ignited controversy for its message about women's rights. Later plays such as *Lady from the Sea* (1888) and *Hedda Gabler* (1890) show a more symbolic and psychological writing style. In 1891, Ibsen returned to Oslo, where he wrote his last four plays.

sociology, and psychology. Women writers became prominent, including Sigrid Undset, Cora Sandel, and Inger Hagerup. Some writers analyzed Nazism and the factors that drew people to it. Knut Hamsun (1859–1952) won the 1920 Nobel Prize for Literature.

Writing in the 1970s showed a political trend, dealing with issues such as social and gender equality. In the 1980s and 1990s, the trend was toward science fiction and fantasy and away from overt discussion of social issues.

Several current Norwegian writers have achieved global attention. These include novelist Per Petterson, Linn Ullmann (daughter of Norwegian actor-director Liv Ullmann and famous Swedish movie director Ingmar Bergman), and journalist Åsne Seierstad, as well as crime fiction writer Jo Nesbø.

## FILM

Norwegians have been making films since the early twentieth century but have been slower to achieve international recognition than their Scandinavian neighbors in Sweden and Denmark. In the 1980s and 1990s, some Norwegian film directors began cooperating with international filmmakers to produce action films with an international orientation. Also, in 1987, Nils Gaup directed *Veiviseren* (*Pathfinder*), the first film to be directed by a Sami in the Sami language. *Pathfinder* was nominated for an Academy Award for Best Foreign Film in 1988—only the third Norwegian film ever nominated. Norwegian film success has continued through the first decade of the twenty-first century.

Today, Norwegians show their love of the cinema by hosting two important film festivals every year. The Norwegian International Film Festival is held in Haugesund in late August. Despite its name, this festival features innovative new films by Norwegian directors. The country's national film awards, the Amandas, are presented here. And in October, the Bergen International Film Festival features subtitled films from around the world.

**Norway's national symbol is the lion.**

## ARTS AND ARCHITECTURE

The "father of Norwegian painting" was Johan Christian Dahl (1788–1857), who painted nature scenes recording Norway's dramatic

**The Scream by Edvard Munch on display in the Munch Museum in Oslo**

scenery. One of his most famous paintings, *Birch in Storm* (1849), depicts the birch tree, often used as a symbol of Norway. A student of Dahl's, Peder Balke, sold a number of oil paintings of north Norwegian landscapes and seascapes to King Louis Philippe of France; these paintings now hang in the Louvre art museum in Paris, France.

From the 1870s on, painting moved more toward realism, with one group, led by Erik Werenskiold, tending toward nationalistic themes. These included everything from illustrations of folktales to realistic landscapes. The other group, led by Christian Krohg, was more international in scope. Krohg was a lawyer and author as well as an artist, and he engaged in social criticism in all three fields.

By far the most famous of Norway's artists is Edvard Munch (1863–1944). He began as a naturalistic painter, but his later works depict emotions and experiences. One of Munch's important works is a cycle of paintings titled *Frieze of Life—A Poem about Life, Love, and Death*. He painted several versions of his most famous painting, *The Scream* (1893).

Norway's earliest architecture began with Viking-built longhouses and progressed during medieval times to wooden stave and then stone churches. From the fifteenth to eighteenth centuries, many buildings were constructed with logs notched on the undersides so they fit tightly together.

One of Norway's most outstanding architectural wonders is Oslo's Opera House. Another is the Arctic Cathedral in Tromsø, whose structure and huge stained glass window suggest Arctic crevasses and

## STEALING A MUNCH

On February 12, 1994, thieves broke a window and used wire cutters to enter Oslo's National Gallery. They removed one version of Munch's masterpiece *The Scream*, leaving a note: "Thanks for the poor security."[5] Three months later, the painting was found undamaged in a hotel south of Oslo. Three Norwegians were arrested. Then, on August 22, 2004, two masked thieves walked into the Munch Museum in daylight, threatened a guard, and removed another version of *The Scream* plus another Munch painting, *The Madonna*. The paintings were uninsured because museum officials considered them "priceless."[6] The paintings were recovered after two years and nine days. Security has now been tightened around both galleries.

the glowing aurora borealis. Czech glass chandeliers resemble icicles hanging from the ceiling.[7] The Sami Parliament building in Karasjok was influenced by the traditional *lavvo* tents, similar to Native American tepees, used by Sami herders for generations. Finally, the Viking Ship Sports Arena in Hamar, in which speed skating races were held during the 1994 Lillehammer Winter Olympics, evokes the shape and size of an upturned Viking ship.

## NORWAY'S STAVE CHURCHES

Of the 2,000 wooden stave churches built from the twelfth into the fourteenth century, only 28 still exist, all in the region south of Trondheim.[8] The largest and one of the most beautiful is the Heddal Stave Church, located along the Telemark Canal in southern Norway. Another is located near the village of Grip, on a tiny island north of Kristiansund. Stave churches vary in size and degree of decoration, but all are constructed the same way. The church has a stone foundation covered with a wooden sill. Staves, or poles, rest on the sill, supporting the walls and roof. The walls are vertical planks, and the roof is wooden shingles coated in pine tar. A few stave churches have been reconstructed. Two of those are the Urnes Stave Church, the oldest and a UNESCO World Heritage Site, and the Borgund Stave Church, which is the best preserved, located at the eastern end of Sogn Fjord.

**Heddal is the largest stave church in Norway.**

# CHAPTER 7
# POLITICS: A SPIRIT OF COOPERATION

Norwegians have a long history of cooperation. In earlier times, cooperating with others was necessary for survival in a harsh, isolated environment. Later, this same instinct helped ensure fairness and equality for every citizen. Norwegians believe strongly in taking collective responsibility for the good of society. Since the 1930s, the country has built a strong social welfare state for this purpose. Education, health care, and social security are equally available to all citizens, and those with higher incomes pay higher taxes to ensure that less successful people have these benefits. Laws are sometimes passed to ensure equality. For example, Norway is considered a world leader in gender equality. Laws ensure women are adequately represented in government and corporate boards and protect the rights of pregnant women and new mothers.

**The Storting, Norway's national parliament, meets in Oslo.**

## NORWAY'S POLITICAL PARTIES IN 2009

| Party | Percent of Vote | No. of Seats |
|---|---|---|
| Labor Party | 35.1 | 64 |
| Progress Party | 22.9 | 41 |
| Conservative Party | 17.2 | 30 |
| Socialist Left Party | 6.2 | 11 |
| Center Party | 6.2 | 11 |
| Christian People's Party | 5.5 | 10 |
| Liberal Party | 3.9 | 2 |
| Other | 2.7 | 0[1] |

# SYSTEM OF GOVERNMENT

Norway, officially known as the Kingdom of Norway, is a constitutional monarchy; that is, it has a king or queen whose powers are limited by the country's constitution and laws. Similar to many democracies, Norway has three branches of government: executive, legislative, and judicial. Laws are made by the government's legislative branch, or parliament, called the Storting. According to the constitution, power resides with the people, who elect the Storting.

The government, or executive branch, is closely connected with the legislative branch, because the head of government, the prime minister, is also the head of the majority party in the legislature. The monarch technically has veto power over the legislature, but this power has not been used since the union with Sweden was dissolved in 1905. The third branch, or judiciary, is relatively independent. It has the political functions of monitoring executive and legislative powers and implementing legislation adopted by the Storting.

**Norway's flag consists of a blue cross, outlined in white, on a red background.**

Norway operates under the constitution adopted May 17, 1814, as Norway was being transferred from Danish to Swedish rule. On June 7, 1905, Norway declared its union with Sweden dissolved and on October 26, 1905, the Swedish king abdicated. Since that time, Norway has been an independent country, but its constitution (except for a number of amendments) has remained the same. The constitution can be amended by a two-thirds majority vote of the legislature.[2]

Norwegians are very invested in their government. All citizens aged 18 and over are eligible to vote, and voter turnout for elections is usually around 80 percent.[3] Similar to many parliamentary countries, Norway has a multiparty system. Those parties receiving the largest number of votes rule by forming a coalition government, in which they compromise on issues and principles and share power.

## THE LEGISLATIVE BRANCH

**Norway belongs to 70 international organizations.**

The legislative branch consists of the Storting, a unicameral parliament established by the constitution in 1814. Since the establishment of parliamentary government in 1884, the Storting has been the highest political body in Norway. At this time, Norway was still under Swedish control and, although the Storting made laws, ultimate control resided with a Swedish, not a Norwegian, king until independence in 1905. The Storting's 169 members are elected to four-year terms by popular vote with proportional representation; that is, each of the country's 19 counties elects a specific number of representatives based on its population and geographic size. It has two major functions: enacting

**Norway's prime minister and Labor Party leader Jens Stoltenberg speaks in downtown Oslo during the Norwegian general elections of 2009.**

legislation and approving the national budget. The executive branch introduces most proposals, which are then voted on by the Storting. The Storting also monitors the executive branch. It can call for a vote of confidence, which is a formal vote to determine how many parliament members support the prime minister. It may also call for a vote of impeachment or set up sessions during which Storting members can directly question the government.

Another legislative body, the Sami People's Congress, was formed in 1989. This body is elected by the Sami people to protect Sami traditions. It has independent control in some matters, such as land use in areas where Sami live.

## THE EXECUTIVE BRANCH

The executive branch of Norway's government consists of the chief of state (King Harald V, since January 17, 1991), the head of government (Prime Minister Jens Stoltenberg, since October 17, 2005), and the Council of Ministers. The monarch's position is hereditary and largely ceremonial but is very important symbolically as the head of state and the representative of Norway to the world. The monarch unifies the country in times of national crisis, as King Haakon VII did during World War II. The prime minister and council are nominally chosen by the monarch but with the approval of the Storting. The prime minister is

**The Sami Parliament of Norway meets in the Plenary Assembly Hall. The building's peaks resemble the tepees the Sami used as nomads.**

## NORWAY'S ROYAL FAMILY

King Harald V succeeded to the throne upon the death on January 17, 1991, of his father, King Olaf V, who had served since 1957. King Harald is the grandson of King Haakon VII, who served from Norway's independence in 1905 through 1957 and saw the country through World War II. The king has two older sisters, Princess Ragnhild, who died in 2012, and Princess Astrid. On August 29, 1968, King Harald married commoner Sonja Haraldsen. They have two children, Princess Märtha Louise (born 1971) and Crown Prince Haakon (born 1973). On August 25, 2001, Prince Haakon married Mette-Marit Tjessem Høiby, now Crown Princess Mette-Marit. Their two children are Princess Ingrid Alexandra (born 2004) and Prince Sverre Magnus (born 2005). The family also includes Prince Haakon's stepson, Marius Borg Høiby, who is Princess Mette-Marit's son by a previous relationship. The Norwegian constitution was amended so that, for children born in or after 1990, the firstborn child succeeds to the throne. Thus, Princess Ingrid is second in line after her father, Crown Prince Haakon, and her younger brother Prince Sverre is third in line.

usually the leader of the majority party or majority coalition in the Storting. Norway's executive branch, particularly the prime minister, has less power than in many parliamentary democracies.

Norwegians have a long tradition of monarchy. Their first king, Harald I, was crowned more than 1,000 years ago. From 1381 to 1814, they were part of a union with Denmark and from 1814 to 1905, a union with Sweden. During those years, they were ruled by Danish and Swedish kings. In 1905, when Norway declared independence, the people chose a new king, Haakon VII, who was born a Danish prince. This succession continues today.

Today's king, Harald V, was the first prince born in Norway in 567 years.

## THE JUDICIAL BRANCH

The third branch of Norway's government is the judiciary. Courts consist of the Supreme Court of Justice, the Interlocutory Appeals Committee of the Supreme Court, the courts of appeals, the district courts, the conciliation courts, and special courts.

Before civil cases are taken to court, they are typically sent to conciliation councils and often settled informally. These decisions can be appealed through the more formal courts of appeals. The nation's final arbiter of justice is the Supreme Court, whose justices are appointed by the king. When citizens have differences with members of the government or its bureaucracy, they may also complain to a special commissioner whose job it is to guard citizens' civil rights.

### NORWAY'S FLAG

Norway's flag has the colors red, white, and blue. The background is red. A blue cross outlined in white extends to the edges of the flag, and the vertical segment of the cross is closer to the hoist side. The colors combine those of the Danish and Swedish flags, recalling Norway's past unions with these countries.

Norway's King Harald V, flanked by Queen Sonja and Crown Prince Haakon, *right*, delivers the government's opening speech during the official opening of the Storting in 2010.

## LOCAL GOVERNMENT

Norway has 19 counties, called *fylker*. Each fylke has a governor appointed by the king meeting with the Council of Ministers. Each of the country's 429 municipalities has an elected council and a mayor.

The powers of these local governments come from the national government through legislation, rather than from the constitution. Municipalities are responsible for primary and lower secondary education, social services, roads, water, sewage, and zoning regulations. Counties are responsible for upper secondary schools and various technical services.

## NORWAY IN THE WORLD

Norway has been a leader in the area of peace and reconciliation and in the fight against injustice, oppression, discrimination, and poverty around the world. The country is strongly committed to building democracy, championing human rights, and challenging unequal distribution of power both within and among countries.

**The first secretary-general of the United Nations was Trygve Lie, a Norwegian.**

To these ends, Norway is a founding member and active participant in many international organizations. These include the United Nations, the North Atlantic Treaty Organization (NATO), the Council of Europe, and the Organization for Security and Cooperation in Europe (OSCE). Each of these organizations, in its own way and within its own jurisdiction, promotes peace, justice, human rights, democracy, security, and the rule of law for its member nations.

A major challenge facing the Norwegian government is the issue of immigration. Despite their traditional ideas of fairness and equality, many native Norwegians are increasingly concerned about the changes

## THE NOBEL PEACE PRIZE

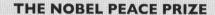

When Swedish industrialist Alfred Nobel conceived of the Nobel Prizes before his death in 1896, Sweden and Norway were still a single union. But Norway's Storting had already distinguished itself through practical policies supporting peace, including disarmament and settling conflicts by arbitration instead of war. Thus, although the other four Nobel Prizes are awarded each year in Stockholm, Sweden, Nobel chose to have the Peace Prize awarded in Oslo. The Norwegian Nobel Institute, founded in 1904, compiles information about nominees. The Storting appoints the five members of the Norwegian Nobel Committee, who choose the recipient. They may award the Peace Prize to individuals, organizations, or groups of up to three individuals associated with the same cause. The Nobel Peace Prize has been called "the world's most prestigious prize awarded for the preservation of peace."[4]

immigrants are bringing to their country. They are particularly concerned about increasing crime rates and abuse of the welfare system. The country's first recorded instance of racially motivated crime occurred in 2001. Political parties are polarized over this issue. In 2005, the Progress Party, which advocates very strict controls on immigration, became the second-largest party in the country. This party blames increasing crime rates on immigrants. Other parties have denounced this characterization as xenophobic.

# STRUCTURE OF THE GOVERNMENT OF NORWAY

| Executive Branch | Legislative Branch | Judicial Branch |
|---|---|---|
| Monarch<br><br>Prime Minister<br><br>Council of Ministers | Storting | Supreme Court of Justice (Høyesterett)<br><br>Interlocutory Appeals Committee of the Supreme Court (Høyesteretts ankeutvalg)<br><br>Courts of Appeals (Lagmannsretten)<br><br>District Courts (tingrett)<br><br>Conciliation Courts (forliksrådet) |

# CHAPTER 8
# ECONOMICS: SHARING THE WEALTH

Norway's prosperity is based on both its abundant natural resources and its ability to exploit them carefully and thoughtfully. Norwegians have tried to use their country's resources to improve their standard of living while still preserving the beauty and health of the environment. They have developed a strong, prosperous economy for this generation while also planning and investing for future generations. They have carefully based their economy on a variety of resources. When North Sea oil was discovered in the late 1960s, it would have been easy to rely entirely on oil revenues. Instead, Norway built up various industries, including fishing, hydropower, lumbering, farming, and mining.

In 2010, Norway had approximately 4.8 million tourists.

**An oil rig supply boat docks at Bergen Harbor.**

## THE NORWEGIAN GOVERNMENT PENSION FUND GLOBAL

When Norway's oil profits began rolling in, the country took a practical approach to handling the money. First, it built up the country's infrastructure, repairing war damage and adding roads, telephones, and more recently, a telecommunications network and other systems necessary for a modern society. Then, it paid off the national debt. In 1996, when Norway was debt free, it established the Norwegian Petroleum Fund, investing enough money to pay for the health and pension costs of coming generations of Norwegians. The plan succeeded brilliantly. In 2006, when the fund's name was changed to the Norwegian Government Pension Fund Global, it was worth approximately US$449 billion. In 2011, it was more than $500 billion, and by 2014, it was expected to reach $765 billion. Fund managers follow strict guidelines. First, they only invest outside Norway, making them one of the largest investors in the world. Second, they practice ethically and socially responsible investment. They refuse to invest in companies or countries accused of human rights violations or severe environmental damage.[2]

Much of the industrial sector is privately controlled, but the government controls the petroleum sector through extensive regulations and enterprises that are majority owned by the government. Petroleum provides the largest share of the country's export revenue, representing approximately 50 percent of the total export value. It provides 20 percent of government revenue and also makes Norway's extensive social safety net possible.[1]

## NORWAY'S ECONOMY TODAY

Because of its relative wealth, Norway survived

**Norwegian currency is the krone.**

recent world economic problems with less difficulty than most other European countries. Its unemployment rate has remained low at approximately 3.3 percent as of 2011, and social programs remain well funded.[3] A country's wealth is measured by its gross domestic product (GDP), or the total value of all goods and services produced in that country in one year. Norway's GDP grew from 2004 through 2007, slowed in 2008, and contracted slightly in 2009; however, in 2010–2011, economic growth resumed. Norway paid off its national debt in 1995, and has had a large budget surplus since that date, even during the recent recession.[4]

## NORWAY'S GDP BY ACTIVITY (2010)

| Economic Activity | Percentage of GDP |
|---|---|
| Oil and gas | 20 |
| General government | 16 |
| Manufacturing, mining, electricity, building, and construction | 15 |
| Value added tax | 11 |
| Commodities, vehicle repairs | 7 |
| Communication and transportation | 4 |
| Agriculture, forestry, and fishing | 2 |
| Other services (commercial, housing, financial, private health/education, hotel and catering, etc.) | 25[7] |

Norway's oil industry quickly transformed the country from one of Europe's poorest countries to one of its richest. In 2011, Norway was the world's seventh-largest oil-exporting country and second-largest natural gas exporter.[5] In the same year, it made another very large offshore oil discovery. Only 0.4 percent of Norway's own electricity comes from fossil fuels—more than 99 percent is produced by renewable sources, mostly hydropower.[6] But through its huge oil exports, the country contributes significantly to greenhouse gas emissions and climate change. Norwegians are well aware of the contradiction between their commitment to environmental sustainability and their burgeoning oil industry. To decrease the impact of oil, Norway has developed a national plan to become carbon neutral by 2050. This means the country plans to achieve a zero net emission of greenhouse gases into the atmosphere by either reducing gas emissions or offsetting them in some way.

## THE BASIS OF NORWAY'S ECONOMY

Norway's natural resources include copper, fish, hydropower, iron ore, lead, natural gas, nickel, petroleum, pyrites, timber, titanium, and zinc. The petroleum and gas industries, including refineries, and mining operations are the major sources of income. Associated with the petroleum industry are large petrochemical and fertilizer industries. Electronics, fisheries, hydroelectric power, shipbuilding, timber, transport equipment, and pulp and paper are other important industries. Although only approximately 2.7 percent of Norway's land is arable, agriculture is a thriving and vital part of the economy.[8] Major agricultural products include dairy, fish, fur, grains, livestock, pork, veal, wool, potatoes and other vegetables, and fruit and berries.

Norway exports more than it imports. Its major exports are metals, chemicals, ships, fish, petroleum and petroleum products, and machinery and equipment. The country also imports machinery and equipment, as well as chemicals, metals, and foodstuffs.

In terms of percentage of GDP, Norway is a service economy, with 57.7 percent of its income in 2011 due to services.[9] Services

**Fishermen sort fresh cod, ready for exporting, in Myre in northern Norway.**

encompass a broad range of activities, including construction, retail sales, transportation, aviation, telecommunications, hotels and restaurants, and health and education services. Norway's spectacular scenery makes tourism a small but important part of the service economy. In 2011, for example, more than 236,000 people visited Norway's North Cape (Nordkapp), Europe's most northern point, many of them to experience the midnight sun.[10]

## INDEPENDENCE AND COOPERATION

Because Norway spent so many centuries under foreign rule, the country guards its independence. Norway voted against membership in the European Union (EU) in both 1972 and 1994. Although the government favored membership, citizens feared it would lead to loss of national sovereignty and negatively affect small businesses, including fisheries and family farms.

Although fiercely independent, Norway does have strong ties to its Scandinavian neighbors. In 1952, it joined the Nordic Council, which also includes Denmark, Sweden, Finland, Iceland, Greenland, and the Faroe Islands. This council enables these far northern countries to cooperate on issues that affect all of them. They develop plans for environmental protection and share health and educational services across country boundaries with minimum bureaucracy.

The nation also maintains close economic ties to its European neighbors as a member of groups including Schengen and the European

## THE FISHERIES INDUSTRY

Fisheries form the basis of Norway's coastal economy. Norway is the world's tenth-largest fishing nation, and fishery products are its third-largest export, after oil/gas and metals. They account for 5.7 percent of its total export value. In 2011, 10,235 people listed fishing as their main occupation, down from more than 68,000 in 1950. Centuries of overfishing have depleted many fish stocks, including herring, cod, and mackerel. After conservation measures began in the 1970s, stocks began to recover, but some populations (particularly cod) will take many years to return to normal. The depletion of wild fish stocks led to the rise of aquaculture. In 2011, 5,333 people were employed in aquaculture, mostly growing pen-raised trout and salmon.[11]

## TOP IMPORT AND EXPORT PARTNERS (2011)

| Exports | | Imports | |
|---|---|---|---|
| **Country** | **Percent of Exports** | **Country** | **Percent of Imports** |
| United Kingdom | 27.2 | Sweden | 13.4 |
| Netherlands | 11.6 | Germany | 12 |
| Germany | 11.1 | China | 9 |
| France | 7 | Denmark | 6.3 |
| Sweden | 6.5 | United Kingdom | 5.6 |
| United States | 5.6 | United States | 5.4[12] |

Economic Area (EEA). The purpose of the Schengen Agreement of 1985 is to allow freedom of movement through all member countries. Once visitors pass through an external border check, they may travel freely within any Schengen country. The agreement sets common rules for external border checks, visas, and refugee rights. To maintain security while still providing freedom of movement, the Schengen area has developed the Schengen Information System (SIS). This database allows member countries to exchange information on potentially dangerous

**Resources of Norway**

Legend:
- Cereals
- Fishing
- Hydroelectric Power
- Livestock
- Manufacturing
- Oil and Gas
- Reindeer
- Timber

## MAJOR SECTORS OF THE ECONOMY

| Sector | Percent of GDP | Percent of Labor Force |
| --- | --- | --- |
| Agriculture | 2.6 | 2.9 |
| Industry | 39.7 | 21.1 |
| Services | 57.7 | 76[14] |

visitors. Schengen has 25 member states (including Norway); 22 are EU members. By easing travel across European borders, Schengen membership is good for both business and tourism.

As of 2012, 30 countries are members of the EEA. The EEA agreement became effective on January 1, 1994. When considering economic questions, the member states act together as if they are a single country. Countries joining the EU are bound by the EEA agreement, which allows for "the free movement of goods, services, persons and capital" throughout the member states.[13] It also allows cooperation in broader areas, including tourism, culture, education, social policy, environmental and consumer protection, and research and development.

Today, Norway is a wealthy, modern society, but the change to wealth and industrialization has occurred rapidly and late in its history. Thus, although Norwegians enjoy their newfound wealth, they still

**Modern trains transport goods and people across Norway.**

retain their strongly individualistic, self-reliant nature. They respect the environment and place a high value on family, friends, and rural life. They are not consumed by work, as is often true in other developed countries. They work hard for 37.5 to 40 hours per week but leave immediately at the end of the workday.[15] They view overtime with suspicion and value after-work leisure time. Norwegians are allotted 35 vacation days per year and 20 private and 15 public holidays.[16] Given their short workweek and long vacations, Norwegians work, on average, only 1,425 hours per year while the average European works 1,700 hours per year.[17] Always quietly active on the world stage, Norway has recently become a more diverse and multicultural state itself, with the influx of immigrants—both refugees and specialized workers needed in the growing economy.

## CHAPTER 9
# NORWAY TODAY

Most Norwegians rise early and are at work at 8:00 a.m. For children, school begins between 8:30 and 9:10. Both children and adults bring a lunch from home, called a *matpakke*. Schools do not have cafeterias, and workers seldom eat lunch out. The length of the school day varies according to the day of the week. Some days, students go home as early as 1:00 p.m., while other days can last as late as 3:30 p.m. Before- and after-school programs are available for all students in grades one through four, and up to grade seven for children with special needs. Adults leave work promptly at 4:00 p.m. The family eats a hot meal at 5:00 or 6:00 p.m.

Evenings are a time for family activities or for participation in clubs or sports. Schedules vary by season. In the winter, when there is little light and they must be up early for work or school, many Norwegians go to bed early. But in the summer, they make the most of the long days. Children play outside until late in the evening, and adults participate in

**A group of teenage friends and skateboarders relaxes in the town of Sortland, Norway.**

## NORWAY'S ATTITUDES TOWARD CHILDREN

Norway is a very child-friendly society. However, traditionally kids are not spoiled; they learn to take care of themselves and quickly become independent and self-reliant. They get to school on their own, often from first grade. Children have safe routes to walk or cycle to school—including sidewalks, cycle tracks, bridges, underpasses, and pedestrian crossings. Speed bumps keep traffic slow, and children have the right to stop traffic by putting out their hand. After school, they spend time in neighborhood play areas and sports facilities.

sports or socialize with friends and family long into the night.

## EDUCATION

Norwegian children are required to receive ten years of education, from ages six to 15 (grades one through ten). This is primary and lower secondary education. Preschool is available for all children younger than school age (ages one through five). In 2010, 89.3 percent of eligible children attended preschool. Because so many children attend preschool for one or more years, adjustment to school can be difficult for those who do not attend. This is especially true for minority or immigrant children whose first language is not Norwegian. Local authorities are required to offer before- and after-school child care for grades one to four. Nearly all schools are fully state-funded public

**Children dance in costumes at the Norwegian Folk Museum at Bygdoy.**

## PARTY TIME FOR SENIORS

From sometime in April to May 17, Norway's high school seniors go a little crazy. Called *Russ*, they engage in several weeks of nonstop partying before their exams. Everyone wears a costume consisting of baggy overalls color coded with the students' course of study (mostly red for general studies) and a beret. The beret has dangling strings filled with knots or figurines, each representing a prank or dare completed. Some pranks are silly or funny, such as sitting under the desk during class; others may be illegal and dangerous. In past generations, Russ celebrations were modest and much shorter, lasting days instead of weeks. But today's wealthy teenagers spend thousands of dollars, often buying and decorating vans or old school buses and driving them around the country celebrating. The party ends on May 17, when the Russ participate in their local Constitution Day parade.

schools. Approximately 2 percent are private.[1]

For the first several years of primary school, emphasis is on socialization and grades are not given, only written evaluations. Subjects taught in primary and lower secondary school include Norwegian, math, social studies, nature studies, English, music, physical education, arts and crafts, second and third foreign languages, food and health, and religion, life view, and ethics (RLE). Children usually begin learning English in first grade.

Upper secondary school provides three years of general education or four years of vocational

**Students about to graduate from high school, called *Russ*, celebrate in special overalls and hats.**

**Norwegians begin learning English in their first year of primary school.**

training, including one or two years of apprenticeship or practical training in an industry. This level is not compulsory and students must apply for admission based on their grades from lower secondary school. Students may choose one of three programs leading to college admission: music, dance, and drama; sports and physical education; or general studies. They may also choose a vocational program such as agriculture, forestry, fisheries, or building and construction. Normally, students attend upper secondary school from ages 16 to 19, but they may attend up to age 25. In 2008, 78 percent of adult Norwegians had completed upper secondary school.[2]

Education beyond the upper secondary level begins after 13 years of school, at approximately age 19, and includes either university or advanced vocational programs. University bachelor's degrees take three years, master's degrees take two years, and PhD degrees take approximately three. Advanced vocational programs last from six months to two years and may be offered by either private or public institutions, usually county authorities.

Norway has a 100 percent literacy rate.[3] However, one cause for concern in Norwegian schools is low performance on international tests, particularly math. Some claim Norwegian schools are too free and relaxed; others point out the schools emphasize independent critical thinking rather than rote learning. Achievement differences also occur within Norwegian schools. Not surprisingly, children from wealthier, better-educated families outperform those from families with lower economic and educational standing. Native Norwegians also outperform immigrant children. Girls—both Norwegian and immigrant—outperform boys in school, and a higher percentage of girls attend university and study abroad.

## NORWAY IN TRANSITION

With wealth from the oil industry and an influx of refugees and workers from around the world, Norway's traditional ways are inevitably changing. Harsh environments with difficult transportation and communication are giving way to dependable transportation systems, cell phones, and computers. Norwegians are highly connected to each other and to the rest of the world. They watch satellite television, chat with friends on social networking sites such as Facebook, spend winter vacations in warm climates, and otherwise take advantage of their wealth to become a globalized nation. Some fear these changes may decrease traditional Norwegian hardiness and self-reliance. Some also fear excess wealth is making life too easy and eroding other characteristics by which Norwegians define themselves—such as cooperation, generosity, responsibility, and respect and consideration for others. Another fear is the loss of social equality, as the wealth of the richest Norwegians is growing noticeably faster than that of the rest of the population.

**Ninety percent of 10-year-olds in Norway have cell phones.**

## THE UNTHINKABLE: MASSACRE ON UTØYA ISLAND

A massacre of 69 teenagers would be an unthinkable tragedy anywhere. In Norway, an extremely peaceful country with a low rate of violent crime, it was doubly shocking. On July 22, 2011, Anders Behring Breivik first set off a car bomb near government buildings in Oslo. After killing eight people, he moved to nearby Utøya Island, where a Labor Party youth camp was in progress. He got onto the island dressed as a policeman and began shooting. Terrified teenagers begged for their lives, tried to hide, or jumped into the water to escape. Before he was stopped, 69 young people, most of them 14 to 17 years old, were dead. Breivik, a right-wing extremist, said he was "defending Norway from multiculturalism."[5] On August 24, 2012, a court found Breivik sane and criminally responsible for the murders and sentenced him to Norway's maximum 21 years in prison. His sentence was for preventive detention, meaning it can be extended if he is considered a danger to the public; thus, he is unlikely ever to be released.

Norway has always been a very safe country. Crime rates are extremely low compared to the United States. For example, in 2009, Norway had 0.6 murders per 100,000 people, while the United States had five per 100,000—more than eight times as many.[4] But in recent years, crime has been increasing. Most common are burglaries, petty theft, pickpocketing, and the selling of counterfeit or pirated goods. These crimes are most likely to occur in the tourist areas of larger cities such as Oslo. With the increase in immigrants and the opening of borders by the Schengen Agreement, organized crime including theft, drugs, and credit

**Flowers commemorate the victims of the massacre in Oslo and Utøya Island in 2011.**

card fraud is also on the rise. Much of this crime involves visitors from Eastern European countries, primarily Bulgaria, Lithuania, and Romania. Finally, there have been several high-profile murder cases, most recently the July 22, 2011, slaughter of 69 teenagers at a camp on Utøya Island. These rare cases are profoundly shocking to this highly peaceful society.

In the past, Norwegians have participated fully in world affairs, often by negotiation and by leaving their country to help solve problems elsewhere. But better communication technology and transportation are changing that. Now the rest of the world is coming to Norway, through tourism, immigration, and technology. The country may never again be quite so safe, but it is becoming more culturally diverse. Although the changes are causing some insecurity, most people are adapting and—in true Norwegian fashion—coming to accept and appreciate the new people and new cultures within their midst.

**Norwegians have joined their country's natural potential with modern infrastructure to prepare for a bright future.**

# [ TIMELINE ]

| | |
|---|---|
| **10,000 BCE** | Ancestors of the Sami people migrate to Norway from the east and the south, following the receding ice. |
| **793 CE** | The Vikings attack the Lindisfarne monastery off England, beginning their rise to power. |
| **890** | Harald I defeats other Viking chieftains to become Norway's first king. |
| **995** | Olaf I Tryggvason tries unsuccessfully to Christianize Norway. |
| **1015** | Olaf II Haraldsson founds Norway's first national government and imposes Christianity on the Norwegian people. |
| **1066** | Harald III Sigurdsson is defeated and killed in a raid on England, marking the end of the Viking supremacy. |
| **1349** | Bubonic plague reaches Norway, eventually killing two-thirds of the population and 80 percent of the nobility. |
| **1397** | The Kalmar Union unites Norway, Sweden, and Denmark. |
| **1523** | Sweden leaves the Kalmar Union, leaving Norway and Denmark united. |
| **1814** | On January 14, Denmark is defeated in the Napoleonic Wars and the Treaty of Kiel is signed, giving Norway to Sweden. |
| **1814** | On May 17, the constitution of Norway and Sweden is signed. |
| **1905** | On June 7, Norway's Parliament votes to break from Sweden and declare Norway independent. |

| 1905 | On October 26, the Swedish King, Oskar II, abdicates control over Norway, making Norway an independent country. |
| 1913 | Norwegian women gain the right to vote. |
| 1914–1918 | Norway remains neutral during World War I. |
| 1940 | On April 9, the German Army invades Norway, forcing the nation into World War II. |
| 1945 | Norway is liberated from German occupation. |
| 1945 | Norway becomes a founding member of the United Nations; Trygve Lie of Norway becomes the first secretary-general. |
| 1952 | Norway joins the Nordic Council. |
| 1964 | The Norwegian constitution is amended to guarantee freedom of religion. |
| 1960s | Petroleum and natural gas are discovered in the North Sea off the coast of Norway, leading to a rapid rise in Norwegian prosperity. |
| 1972 | Norway first votes against membership in the European Union, which was called the European Economic Community at the time. |
| 1991 | On January 17, King Harald V succeeds to the throne following the death of his father, King Olaf V. |
| 1996 | Norway establishes the Norwegian Petroleum Fund, later renamed the Norwegian Government Pension Fund Global. |

# FACTS AT YOUR FINGERTIPS

## GEOGRAPHY

Official name: Kingdom of Norway; short form: Norway

Area: 125,021 square miles (323,802 sq km)

Climate: temperate along coast, warm by North Atlantic Current (Gulf Stream); interior colder with increased precipitation and colder summers; rainy all year on west coast

Highest elevation: Galdhøpiggen, 8,100 feet (2,469 m) above sea level

Lowest elevation: Norwegian Sea, at sea level

Significant geographic features: Norwegian Sea, Scandinavian Mountains

## PEOPLE

Population (July 2012 est.): 4,707,270

Most populous city: Oslo

Ethnic groups: Norwegian, 94.4 percent (includes approximately 40,000 Sami); other European, 3.6 percent; other, 2 percent (2007 estimate)

Percentage of residents living in urban areas: 79 percent

Life expectancy: 80.32 years (world rank: 27)

Languages: Bokmål Norwegian (official), Nynorsk Norwegian (official), small Sami- and Finnish-speaking minorities; Sami is official in six municipalities

Religions: Church of Norway (Evangelical Lutheran), 85.7 percent; Pentecostal, 1 percent; Roman Catholic, 1 percent; other Christian, 2.4 percent; Muslim, 1.8 percent; other, 8.1 percent

## GOVERNMENT AND ECONOMY

Government: constitutional monarchy

Capital: Oslo

Date of adoption of current constitution: May 17, 1814

Head of state: monarch

Head of government: prime minister

Legislature: unicameral parliament, or Storting (169 members)

Currency: Norwegian kroner

Industries and natural resources: Industries include petroleum and gas, food processing, shipbuilding, pulp and paper products, metals, chemicals, timber, mining, textiles,

and fishing. Agricultural products include barley, wheat, potatoes, pork, beef, veal, milk, and fish. Natural resources include petroleum, natural gas, iron ore, copper, lead, zinc, titanium, pyrites, nickel, fish, timber, and hydropower.

# FACTS AT YOUR FINGERTIPS CONTINUED

## NATIONAL SYMBOLS

Holidays: May 17 is Constitution Day, celebrating the signing of the Constitution in 1814

Flag: Red with a blue cross outlined in white that extends to the edges of the flag

National anthem: "Ja, vi elsker dette landet" ("Yes, We Love This Country")

National symbol: lion

## KEY PEOPLE

Harald I, Norway's first king

Harald V, king since 1991

Edvard Munch (1863–1944), artist

Jens Stoltenberg, prime minister since 2005

## COUNTIES (FYLKER) OF NORWAY

**County; Capital**

Akershus; Oslo

Aust-Agder; Arendal

Buskerud; Drammen

Finnmark; Vadsø

Hedmark; Hamar

Hordaland; Bergen

Møre og Romsdal; Molde

Nordland; Bodø

Nord-Trøndelag; Steinkjer

Oppland; Lillehammer

Oslo; City of Oslo

Østfold; Sarpsborg

Rogaland; Stavanger

Sogn og Fjordane; Leikanger

Sør-Trøndelag; Trondheim

Telemark; Skien

Troms; Tromsø

Vest-Agder; Kristiansand

Vestfold; Tønsberg

# GLOSSARY

**aquaculture**
Fish farming.

**archipelago**
A large group of islands clustered in an ocean or sea.

**chantey**
A song sailors sing to keep their work in rhythm.

**coalition government**
A government formed by multiple political parties who must compromise on principles.

**fjord**
A narrow ocean or sea inlet often between steep slopes or cliffs.

**indigenous**
Originating in, or native to, a specific country or region.

**martial law**
Rule by an occupying army.

**permafrost**
Permanently frozen soil found in Arctic tundra regions.

**secular**

Nonreligious.

**skerry**

A tiny island too small to live on.

**tundra**

A type of environment in the far north or at high altitudes that is very cold and has low rainfall, poor drainage, and low plant and animal diversity.

**unicameral**

Having or consisting of a single legislative chamber.

**welfare state**

A political system in which the government is responsible for the welfare of citizens (for example, education, health care, and retirement benefits).

**xenophobic**

Having fear of or contempt for strangers or foreigners.

# ADDITIONAL RESOURCES

## SELECTED BIBLIOGRAPHY

"About Norway." *Norway: The Official Site in the United States*. Royal Norwegian Embassy in Washington, 2012. Web. 1 July 2012.

"Background Note: Norway." *US Department of State*. US Department of State, 20 June 2012. Web. 1 July 2012.

Ham, Anthony, Stuart Butler, and Miles Roddis. *Norway*. Oakland, CA: Lonely Planet, 2011. Print.

March, Linda. *Norway*. London, UK: Kuperard, 2011. Print.

O'Leary, Margaret Hayford. *Culture and Customs of Norway*. Santa Barbara, CA: Greenwood, 2010. Print.

"State of the Environment Norway." *Environment.no*. Environmental Directorates in Norway, 2012. Web. 1 July 2012.

"The World Factbook: Norway." *CIA World Factbook*. Central Intelligence Agency, 20 June 2012. Web. 1 July 2012.

## FURTHER READINGS

Dregni, Eric. *In Cod We Trust: Living the Norwegian Dream*. Minneapolis, MN: U of Minnesota P, 2008. Print.

Gallagher, Thomas Michael. *Assault in Norway: Sabotaging the Nazi Nuclear Program*. Guilford, CT: Lyons Press, 2010. Print.

George, Jessica Day. *Sun and Moon, Ice and Snow*. London: Bloomsbury, 2009. Print.

Peyre, Marie. *Norway*. London: Insight, 2011. Print.

## WEB LINKS

To learn more about Norway, visit ABDO Publishing Company online at **www.abdopublishing.com**. Web sites about Norway are featured on our Book Links page. These links are routinely monitored and updated to provide the most current information available.

## PLACES TO VISIT

*If you are ever in Norway, consider checking out these important and interesting sites!*

### Oslo

Oslo's many museums and landmarks will give you a good flavor of Norway's history and culture. These include the National Museum of Contemporary Art, the Historical Museum, Oslo Cathedral, and Oslo City Museum.

### Svalbard Islands

To view some of Norway's typical wildlife and to see up close the glaciers so characteristic of Norway, visit the island archipelago of Svalbard. In the winter, take a dog-sledding tour; in the summer, boat or snowmobile trips or glacier hikes will lead you to polar bears, arctic foxes, and reindeer.

### Tromsø

The city of Tromsø, far above the Arctic Circle, claims many "northernmost" titles, including the northernmost university, cathedral, brewery, botanic garden, and Burger King restaurant. Tromsø is also an ideal place to experience the midnight sun or the polar night and the aurora borealis.

# SOURCE NOTES

### CHAPTER 1. A VISIT TO NORWAY

1. "Snøhetta. Oslo Opera House, Oslo, Norway." *Arcspace.com*. Arcspace, 21 Apr. 2008. Web. 14 June 2012.

2. "The World's Best Train Ride." *VisitNorway.us*. Innovation Norway, 13 Dec. 2010. Web. 15 June 2012.

### CHAPTER 2. GEOGRAPHY: TOP OF THE WORLD

1. "The World Factbook: Norway." *Central Intelligence Agency*. Central Intelligence Agency, 29 May 2012. Web. 1 June 2012.

2. "Landforms." *Norway Landforms and Land Statistics*. World Atlas, n.d. Web. 6 June 2012.

3. Linda March. *Norway*. London, UK: Kuperard. 2006. Print. 13.

4. "The World Factbook: Norway." *Central Intelligence Agency*. Central Intelligence Agency, 29 May 2012. Web. 1 June 2012.

5. "The World Factbook: Norway." *Central Intelligence Agency*. Central Intelligence Agency, 29 May 2012. Web. 1 June 2012.

6. "Glaciers in Norway." *VisitNorway.us*. Innovation Norway, 24 Jan. 2012. Web. 6 June 2012.

7. "Background Note: Norway." *US Department of State*. US Department of State, 7 March 2012. Web. 7 June 2012.

8. "The World Factbook: Norway." *Central Intelligence Agency*. Central Intelligence Agency, 29 May 2012. Web. 1 June 2012.

9. "Norway Facts." *Norway-hei.com*. Norwei-hei.com, n.d. Web. 6 June 2012.

10 Linda March. *Norway*. London, UK: Kuperard. 2006. Print. 15.

11. "Lake Mjøsa." *Encyclopædia Britannica*. Encyclopædia Britannica, 2012. Web. 6 June 2012.

12. "Glomma." *Encyclopædia Britannica*. Encyclopædia Britannica, 2012. Web. 6 June 2012.

13. Anthony Ham. *Norway*. Oakland, CA: Lonely Planet, 2011. Print. 203–204, 227, 385–386.

14. Linda March. *Norway*. London, UK: Kuperard. 2006. Print. 16.

15. Ibid. 15.

16. "Norway" *Weatherbase*. Canty and Associates, 2012. Web. 2 June 2012.

### CHAPTER 3. ANIMALS AND NATURE: NORTHERN DIVERSITY

1. Bruce Barcott. "Svalbard." *National Geographic*. National Geographic Society, April 2009. Web. 7 July 2012.

2. "Norway: Animals and Plants." *MapZones*. MapZones, 2008. Web. 7 June 2012.

3. Anthony Ham. *Norway*. Oakland, CA: Lonely Planet, 2011. Print. 386–387.

4. Ibid.

5. "Protected Areas." *Environment.no.* Environmental Directorates in Norway, 18 July 2012. Web. 28 July 2012.

6. "Summary Statistics: Summaries by Country, Table 5, Threatened Species in Each Country." *IUCN Red List of Threatened Species.* International Union for Conservation of Nature and Natural Resources, 2010. Web. 2 June 2012.

7. "Protected Areas." *Environment.no.* Environmental Directorates in Norway, 18 July 2012. Web. 28 July 2012.

8. Anthony Ham. *Norway.* Oakland, CA: Lonely Planet, 2011. Print. 357.

**CHAPTER 4. HISTORY: ROAD TO PROSPERITY**

1. Anthony Ham. *Norway.* Oakland, CA: Lonely Planet, 2011. Print. 373–374.

2. Ibid. 375.

3. "Norway." *Encyclopædia Britannica.* Encyclopædia Britannica, 2012. Web. 7 June 2012.

4. Ibid.

5. Ibid.

6. Anthony Ham. *Norway.* Oakland, CA: Lonely Planet, 2011. Print. 51.

7. "Jews in Norway." *Encyclopedia Judaica.* Encyclopedia Judaica, 1971. Web. 29 July 2012.

8. "What the Marshall Plan Did for Norway." *Norway: The Official Site in the United States.* Royal Norwegian Embassy, 1997. Web. 22 June 2012.

9. Anthony Ham. *Norway.* Oakland, CA: Lonely Planet, 2011. Print. 379.

**CHAPTER 5. PEOPLE: VIKING ROOTS**

1. "The World Factbook: Norway." *Central Intelligence Agency.* Central Intelligence Agency, 29 May 2012. Web. 1 June 2012.

2. "Immigration and Immigrants." *Statistics Norway.* Statistics Norway, 2012. Web. 29 July 2012.

3. Anthony Ham. *Norway.* Oakland, CA: Lonely Planet, 2011. Print. 404.

4. "Norway Separates Church and State." *Local: Norway's News in English.* Local, 21 May 2012. Web. 29 July 2012.

5. "The World Factbook: Norway." *Central Intelligence Agency.* Central Intelligence Agency, 29 May 2012. Web. 1 June 2012.

6. "Norway Separates Church and State." *Local: Norway's News in English.* Local, 21 May 2012. Web. 29 July 2012.

7. Anthony Ham. *Norway.* Oakland, CA: Lonely Planet, 2011. Print. 383.

8. Margaret Hayford O'Leary. *Culture and Customs of Norway.* Santa Barbara, CA: Greenwood, 2010. Print. 41, 53.

9. Ibid. 61–62.

10. Anthony Ham. *Norway*. Oakland, CA: Lonely Planet, 2011. Print. 381–382.

11. Ibid.

### CHAPTER 6. CULTURE: FOLK HERITAGE

1. Margaret Hayford O'Leary. *Culture and Customs of Norway*. Santa Barbara, CA: Greenwood, 2010. Print. 158–161.

2. "Holmenkollen Ski Marathon." *VisitNorway.us*. Innovation Norway, 2012. Web. 30 July 2012.

3. "Woman Wins Finnmarksløpet for Second Time." *Barents Observer*. Barents Observer, 16 Mar. 2012. Web. 30 July 2012.

4. Anthony Ham. *Norway*. Oakland, CA: Lonely Planet, 2011. Print. 383.

5. Ibid. 59.

6. Ibid. 59.

7. Ibid. 316.

8. Margaret Hayford O'Leary. *Culture and Customs of Norway*. Santa Barbara, CA: Greenwood, 2010. Print. 185–186.

### CHAPTER 7. POLITICS: A SPIRIT OF COOPERATION

1. "The World Factbook: Norway." *Central Intelligence Agency*. Central Intelligence Agency, 29 May 2012. Web. 1 June 2012.

2. Ibid.

3. Ibid.

4. "The Nobel Peace Prize." *Norway: The Official Site in the United States*. Royal Norwegian Embassy, 2012. Web. 1 July 2012.

### CHAPTER 8. ECONOMICS: SHARING THE WEALTH

1. "The World Factbook: Norway." *Central Intelligence Agency*. Central Intelligence Agency, 29 May 2012. Web. 1 June 2012.

2. Ibid.

3. Ibid.

4. Anthony Ham. *Norway*. Oakland, CA: Lonely Planet, 2011. Print. 379, 381.

5. "The World Factbook: Norway." *Central Intelligence Agency*. Central Intelligence Agency, 29 May 2012. Web. 1 June 2012.

6. "Background Note: Norway." *US Department of State*. US Department of State, 7 March 2012. Web. 7 June 2012.

7. Anthony Ham. *Norway*. Oakland, CA: Lonely Planet, 2011. Print. 378–379, 398–399.

8. "The World Factbook: Norway." *Central Intelligence Agency*. Central Intelligence Agency, 29 May 2012. Web. 1 June 2012.

9. Ibid.

10. "Record-Number of Tourists Visit Nordkapp." *Norway Inspires*. Norway Inspires, n.d. Web. 26 June 2012.

11. "Fishing and Fish Farming." *Statistics Norway*. Statistics Norway, 2012. Web. 30 July 2012.

12. "The World Factbook: Norway." *Central Intelligence Agency*. Central Intelligence Agency, 29 May 2012. Web. 1 June 2012.

13. "EEA Agreement." *European Free Trade Association*. European Free Trade Association, 2012. Web. 25 June 2012.

14. "The World Factbook: Norway." *Central Intelligence Agency*. Central Intelligence Agency, 29 May 2012. Web. 1 June 2012.

15. Linda March. *Norway*. London, UK: Kuperard. 2006. Print. 46.

16. Gus Lubin. "39 Developed Countries with More Vacation Days Than America." *Business Insider*. Business Insider, 1 July 2011. Web. 30 July 2012.

17. Solveig Torvik. "Norway's Economic Riddle." *Views and News from Norway*. Views and News from Norway, 13 May 2011. Web. 30 July 2012.

## CHAPTER 9. NORWAY TODAY

1. Margaret Hayford O'Leary. *Culture and Customs of Norway*. Santa Barbara, CA: Greenwood, 2010. Print. 63.

2. Ibid.

3. "The World Factbook: Norway." *Central Intelligence Agency*. Central Intelligence Agency, 29 May 2012. Web. 1 June 2012.

4. Zaid Jilani. "As The Right Bemoans Norway's Criminal Justice System, It Is One of the Safest Countries on Earth." *Think Progress Justice*. American Progress Action Fund. July 25, 2011. Web. 1 July 2012.

5. "Anders Breivik Describes Norway Island Massacre." *BBC News Europe*. BBC, 20 Apr. 2012. Web. 5 July 2012.

# INDEX

# PHOTO CREDITS